Non Muslims in the
ISLAMIC
SOCIETY

Yusuf al-Qaradawi
Tr. by **Khalil Muhammad Hamad**
Sayed Mahboob Ali Shah

Library of Congress Catalog Card No. 83-072763
ISBN No. 0-89259-049-1

American Trust Publications
10900 W. Washington Street
Indianapolis, Indiana 46231 — USA

Tel: (317) 839-8150
Telex No: 276242 ISLAMIC BS

Printed in the United States of America

CONTENTS

Preface

Praise be to Almighty Allah, and peace and blessings of Allah be upon His Messsenger, the final and noblest of all, Muhammad ibn Abdullah, his household, companions, and followers.

For several centuries the Muslim community has suffered at the hands of colonialists who by imposing on them an alien way of life deprived them of their true personality.

With the return of freedom to Muslim lands, the old war against Islam has, however, not ceased; only its form has changed. Efforts are being made by certain vested interests to thwart the Islamic aspirations of the Muslim *ummah* by raising the issue of non-Muslim minorities which, they claim, will suffer, should the *ummah* return to Islam.

Supported by some ill-intentioned non-Muslim writers they cite occasional cases of mistreatment of the non-Muslim minorities under Muslim rule in the past, forgetting that an aberration cannot detract from the general pattern of Islamic benevolence toward other faiths. They also forget that the lack of Islamic character in some Muslim rulers also led to the oppression of the Muslim majority in the past.

In fact, such exercises are not motivated by a search for truth but by a vicious desire to defame Islam and Muslim history. That there is a need for sifting the truth from falsehood is, therefore, self evident.

In the following pages, we will delineate the teachings of Islam in regard to other faiths; the protection, civil liberties, and honor that Islam gives to non-Muslims; and the obligations that they, in return, owe to the Islamic state. We will also delve into past history to demonstrate the good way of endeavor to erase doubts and suspicions and to enhance the understanding of the subject, especially at a time when hatred among the different religions is being spread, and there are calls for class struggle.

I pray to Almighty Allah that He may open the hearts of the people to accept the truth, and that He may fill their hearts with love, and guide their minds with knowledge and confidence. Verily, Allah is oft-hearing and ready to answer.

Yusuf al-Qaradawi

Introduction To The Translation

All praise to Allah, the Almighty, the Sustainer of all universes. May the peace and blessings of Allah be upon the last of the messengers, Muhammad, his household, and his companions.

We have the privilege of rendering this Arabic book, *Non-Muslims in the Islamic Society*, into English for both Muslim and non-Muslim readers in order to introduce them to this important subject, which has been distorted and misinterpreted by some non-Muslim writers.

This is a research work, based on jurisprudential texts and historical facts. It clarifies the rights and liabilities of *ahl adh-dhimma* (non-Muslims), and the concept of Islamic tolerance and indulgence. It dispels misgivings by placing the facts before the readers. It is a comparative reading of Islam and other faiths on treating minorities.

Throughout his work, Dr. Yusuf al-Qaradawi maintains a lucid style, avoiding tedious interpretations with a firm grip on his subject matter. His intellectual integrity and uncompromising search for facts uniquely qualify him to undertake such an enterprise. Al-Qaradawi is a recognized scholar of the Muslim world. Some of his works have been translated into several languages.

The issue of non-Muslims in an Islamic society, thanks to the adversaries of Islam, carries an undeserved stricture. We hope with the translation of al-Qaradawi's work into English the controversy and misconceptions will give way to a better understanding of the subject. This work is to introduce both Muslims and non-Muslims to the concept of tolerance in Islam, and the role it has to play in these days of Islamic revival throughout the Islamic world.

In our attempt to render this book into English, we have tried not to deviate from the original. As to the meanings of the textual citations from the *Qur'an*, we have mostly relied upon 'Abdullah Yusuf Ali's translation. We have documented all references according to the Arabic text.

We pray to Almighty Allah to make it useful for the readers and to bless its author for writing such a valuable book. May He accept our humble effort in the service of His cause.

Khalil Mohammad Hamad
Sayed Mahboob Ali Shah

Sha'ban 12, 1402 / June 4, 1982

I / Muslim Society - A Society of Belief

Islamic society is based upon a unique faith, from which its systems, rules, arts, and ethics emanate. No wonder the entire life of this society is regulated by Islamic law. This law, the *shari'ah*, is applied to every aspect of Muslim life, individually and socially, materially and spiritually, locally and internationally.

It calls for establishing relations between its Muslim and non-Muslim citizens on a firm basis of tolerance, indulgence, justice, mercy, and virtue. These foundations were not known to mankind before the Islamic era. Even after the advent of Islam, a large part of humanity remained deprived of its blessing. So noble and elusive are these elements of civilized existence that even today modern societies are seeking their actuality. Unfortunately, many times mankind has plunged into bloody conflicts on issues of religious denominations, race, and color.

Regulations of Relationships with Non-Muslims

This relationship is based upon Allah's words in the Qur'an:

> God forbids you not with regard to those who fight you not for (your) faith nor drive you out of your homes, from dealing kindly and justly with them: For God loveth those who are just. God only forbids you with regard to those who fight you for (your) faith and drive you out of your homes and support (others) in driving you out from turning to them (for friendship and protection). It is such as turn to them (in these circumstances) that do wrong. (Al-Mumtahana: 8-9)

According to the Qur'an, a Muslim is required to deal with all people kindly and justly, even with the followers of other faiths, as long as they do not oppose or oppress Muslims, or place obstacles in the way of spreading Islam.

Among non-Muslims, the *people of the book* are those whose religions are based on divine books, the corruption of their books notwithstanding. For example, Judaism is based on the Torah (Old Testament) and Christianity on the Injil (New Testament).

The Qur'an prohibits serious religious discussions with malice and rancor, for they result in hostility, and they arouse prejudice, resentment, and bitter feelings. Allah says:

And do not dispute with the People of the Book except with better means (than mere disputation) unless it be with those who inflict wrong (and injury). But say, 'We believe in the Revelation which has come down to us and in that which came down to you. Our God and your God is one, and it is to Him that we bow (in Islam).' (Al-'Ankabut: 46)

Islam permits Muslims to take meals with the *people of the book*, and to eat their slaughtered animals, as well as to marry their chaste women. The Qur'an further decrees that married life should be established upon love and compassion. As such, it is truly an act of dispensation on the part of Islam that it allows a Muslim to select, if he so desires, his lifelong mate and offspring from among non-Muslim women. Allah says:

The food of the People of the Book is lawful unto you and yours is lawful unto them. (Lawful unto you in marriage) are (not only) chaste women who are believers, but chaste women among the People of the Book revealed before your time — when you give them their due dowers and desire chastity, not lewdness nor secret intrigues.(al-Ma'idah: 5)

This *'ayah* refers to the *people of the book*. Whether they are living in an Islamic state or not is immaterial.

But when they live as non-Muslim citizens under Islamic sovereignty, they enjoy a special status and are known along with other minorities as *ahl adh-dhimma* or *dhimmis*. *Dhimma* is an Arabic word which means safety, security, and contract. Hence, they were called *dhimmis* because they were guaranteed contract by Allah, His Messenger, and the Islamic community. This security granted to *dhimmis* is like the citizenship granted by a government to an alien who abides by the constitution, thereby earning all the rights of a natural citizen. Thus, upon the preceding basis, a *dhimmi* is a citizen of the Islamic state, as described by Muslim jurists,[1] or a bearer of Islamic nationality, as described by contemporary writers.[2] This *dhimmi* contract is everlasting. Nevertheless, this contract is not one-sided; it establishes rights and obligations for both parties, the Muslim government as well as the *dhimmis*. The non-Muslims are extended the security and the protection of the Islamic state provided they pay the *jizyah* (capitation tax) and respect its Islamic constitution. The constitutional conformity, however, does not infringe upon their faith and practices, which remains free in an autonomous entity within the Islamic state.

We will now clarify the rights and obligations of the *ahl adh-dhimma*.

---

[1]See the commentary on As-Sarakhsi's *As-Siyar Al-Kabir*, Vol. I, p. 140; Al-Kasani's *Al-Bada'i'*, Vol. V, p. 281; and Ibn Qudamah's *Al-Mughni*, Vol. V, p. 516.
[2]See 'Awda, 'Abdul Qadir, *Islmaic Criminal Legislation*, Vol. I, p. 307; Zaydan, 'Abdul Karim, "*Ahkam Adh-Dhimmiyyin Wa Al-Musta'minin Fi Dar Al-Islam*," pp. 49-51 and 63-66.

THE RIGHTS OF AHL ADH-DHIMMA

The non-Muslims and the Muslims in *dar al-Islam* (the Islamic state) have equal rights and obligations, except in certain matters.

Right of Protection

They have the right to enjoy the protection of the Islamic state. This right includes protection from outside aggression and inside oppression, so that they may lead a peaceful life.

Protection from Outside Aggression

The non-Muslims and Muslims have equal rights in this connection: the *imam* (ruler of the Muslims), by virtue of the executive and military power granted him by the Islamic *shari'ah*, should provide protection for all of them. It is stated in the Hanbali book of *fiqh* (Islamic religious law), *Matalib Ula An-Nuha:*

> The ruler of the Muslim community is bound to protect the non-Muslims and to save them from aggression. Should they fall into captivity, the *imam* must marshal all the resources to secure their release and punish the transgressors against their lives and properties, even if they were the sole (non-Muslims) living in a remote village.[3]

In his book *Al-Furuq*, Imam Al-Qarafi al-Malaki, quoting from *Maratib Al-Ijma'* by Ibn Hazm, states:

> Muslims who have entered into a pact of *dhimma*, should fight until death with those who try to oppress non-Muslims in the Islamic state in order to abide by the guarantee given to them by Almighty Allah, His messenger, upon whom be peace. Otherwise they will be considered as traitors.

The author takes this decision as the *ijma'* of the Muslim community, a rule accepted by most Muslim scholars (or consensus).

In this connection, Imam Al-Qarafi states:

> "A contract whose fulfillment endangers the lives and property of Muslims who are protecting its subjects (non-Muslims) from harm is indeed a great one."[4]

Ibn Taimiyyah's attitude in this regard provides a living example. He went as an emissary to Qatlo Shah, a Tartar invader of Syria, to negotiate the release of all prisoners of war. The Tartar commander agreed to free the Muslim prisoners but not the non-Muslims. Ibn Taimiyyah, insisted on their release

---

[3]Al-Hanbal, Ahmad Ibn, *Matalib Ula An-Nuha*, Vol. II, pp. 602-603.
[4]Al-Malaki, Imam Al-Qarafi, *Al-Furuq*, Vol. III, p. 15, Farq 119.

because the non-Muslims were under Muslim protection. His persistence paid off, and the non-Muslims were set free.

Protection from Inside Oppression

Protecting the non-Muslims from inside aggression or oppression is a compelling obligation. Islam warns Muslims against showing any aggression, by word or deed, toward the non-Muslims. Allah does not love aggressors, and He does not guide them. He is very swift in bringing them to account in this world, and He will punish them severely in the Hereafter for their transgressions against these people.

There are several Qur'anic verses and prophetic traditions which prohibit aggression, and warn of its repercussions in this world and in that to come, especially if the aggression violates their covenant with the non-Muslims. The Prophet said: "Those who commit an act of aggression against a member of the non-Muslims, who usurp his rights, who make any demand upon him which is beyond his capacity to fulfill, or who forcibly obtain anything from him against his wishes, I will be his (the oppressed's) advocate on the Day of Judgment."[5]

The Prophet also said, "I will be the opponent of one who harms a non-Muslim, and I will speak against those whom I oppose on the Day of Judgement[6]

He said in another tradition, "He who harms a non-Muslim harms me, and he who harms me, harms Allah."[7]

In his contract with the Christians of Najran, the Prophet said, "No man from among them may be held accountable for the violations of another of his fellows."[8]

Because of these prophetic injunctions, Muslims since the early caliphate have been seriously concerned about the protection of non-Muslims from any oppression or ill treatment and have taken care to redress their grievances.

The second *caliph*, 'Umar ibn al-Khattab, used to ask those who came to him from various provinces about the well-being of the non-Muslim citizenry, lest they were facing oppression from anybody; but all of them would acknowledge, "We have witnessed nothing but the fulfillment," — that is, Muslims and non-Muslims were abiding by the conditions of the contract.[9]

'Ali ibn Abi Talib, the fourth *caliph*, said, "They pay capitation tax so that their properties and lives may be as ours."[10]

The *fuqaha'* of the various Islamic legal schools agree that Muslims must protect the non-Muslims from any oppression, and must protect their lives, as they are bound to do for all who live in the Islamic state. Certain *fuqaha'* have even claimed that the sin of oppressing non-Muslims is even worse than

[5]Related by Imams Abu Dawood and Baihaqi in *As-Sunan Al-Kubra*, Vol. V, p. 205.
[6]Related by Al-Khatib, with a good series of transmission.
[7]Related by Imam At-Tabarani in *Al-Awsat*, with a good series of transmission.
[8]Related by Abu Yusuf in *Al-Kharaj*, pp. 72-73.
[9]*Tarikh at-Tabari*, Vol. IV, p. 18.
[10]*Al-Mughni*, Vol. VIII, p. 445; *Al-Bada'i'*, Vol. VII, p. 111 quoting from *Ahkam Adh-Dhimmiyin Wa Al-Musta'minin*, p. 89.

oppressing a Muslim.[11]

Protection of Persons and Lives

Muslims agree that the lives, blood, wealth, and honor of the non-Muslims living among them are inviolate. According to Islamic *ijma'*, it is prohibited and unlawful to kill them. The Prophet, upon whom be peace, said, "He who kills a *mu'ahid*[12] will never smell the fragrance of paradise, the fragrance of which can be smelled from a distance of 40-year travel."[13] That is why the *fuqaha'* agree that the killing of a non-Muslim is a great sin. They are, however, of different opinions about the execution of a Muslim who has killed a non-Muslim owing to the following sound *hadith*: "A Muslim is not killed in lieu of an infidel."[14] Another *hadith* states: "Behold! A Muslim is not killed in lieu of an infidel or a *mu'ahid* (a person who has entered into a covenant with the Muslims)."[15] We will determine the meaning of this hadith in the following:

Imams Malik and Al-Laith said, "A Muslim who intentionally kills a non-Muslim for no reason will be put to death. If his action is justified, he shall not be killed."[16] This is according to Abanah ibn 'Uthman's verdict, who was one of the *fuqaha'* and the governor of Madinah. He sentenced to death a Muslim who had killed a Copt.[17] Imams Ash-Sha'bi, An-Nakha'i, Ibn Abi Laila, 'Uthman al-Betti, Abu Hanifah and their colleagues were of the opinion that a Muslim should be killed if he took the life of a non-Muslim. Their views are based on texts from the *Qur'an* and the *sunnah* (which are general in punitive retaliation, *al-qasas*, and equal in the eternal innocence of blood) as well as a *hadith* which relates that the Prophet, on one occasion when he killed a Muslim in lieu of a mu'ahid, said, "I am the best to fulfill this covenant."[18] Their opinion was also based on the statement that a Muslim who had killed a non-Muslim was brought before 'Ali ibn Abi Talib. After hearing the witnesses' testimony, 'Ali ordered him to be put to death. The deceased's brother came and said, "I have forgiven him." 'Ali said, "Perhaps they have threatened and frightened you." He said, "Not at all, but his death cannot restore my brother's life. They have compensated me, and now I am satisfied." 'Ali said, "You know better. The blood of the person who is in our covenant is like ours and his blood compensation (*diyah*) is like

---

[11]Ibn Abidin said this in his book of commentary the *Hashiya*.

[12]Ibn Al-Athir said, "The term *mu'ahid* is used mostly for *dhimmis* and also for pagans who had entered into a treaty with the Muslims to end a state of war." *Faid Al-Qadir*, Vol. VI, p. 153.

[13]Related by Imams Ahmad and Al-Bukhari in *Jizya*, and by Imams An-Nisa'i and Ibn Majah in *Ad-Diyat*, on the authority of 'Abdullah Ibn 'Amr.

[14]Related by Imams Ahmad, Al-Bukhari, An-Nisa'i, Abu Dawood, and At-Tirmidhi, on the authority of 'Ali. See *Al-Muntaqa* and its commentary, and *Nail Al-Awtar*, Vol. VII, p. 15, ed. Dar Al-Jil Ash-Shabab.

[15]Related by Imams Ahmad, An-Nisa'i, and Abu Dawood, on the authority of 'Ali; elucidated upon by Imam Al-Hakim in *Al-Muntaqa* and its commentary. See previous reference.

[16]*Nail Al-Awtar*, Vol. VII, p. 154.

[17]See *Al-Jawhar An-Naqi* and *As-Sunan Al-Kubra*, Vol. VIII, p. 34.

[18]Related by Imams 'Abdur Razzaq and Al-Baihaqi. Al-Baihaqi says that it is weak. See *As-Sunan*, Vol. VIII, p. 20, and the commentary of Ibn Turkamani in *Al-Jawhar An-Naqi*, "Notes on As-Sunan Al-Kubra." See also *Al-Musannaf*, Vol. X, pp. 101-102.

ours."[19]

In another *hadith*, 'Ali, Allah be pleased with him, stated, "They pay the capitation tax so that their blood and wealth become like our blood and wealth, immune from all harm." 'Umar ibn 'Abdul 'Aziz once wrote to a governor concerning a Muslim who had killed a non-Muslim, telling them to hand the Muslim over to the legal heir of the slain person and to give him the authority either to forgive the Muslim or to kill him. The heir subsequently chose to behead the Muslim.[20]

Thus, in accordance with the same principle, the *fuqaha'* ruled that any Muslim who steals from a non-Muslim would have his hand cut off, although the matter of money is not as crucial as the matter of murder. The Prophet's utterance, "A Muslim is not to be killed in lieu of an infidel," refers to an infidel who fights against Muslims on the battlefield. The *ahadith* on this subject are unanimous.[21] It was this opinion which the Ottoman Empire upheld throughout its widespread territories for centuries, up to its destruction in recent times.

Islam protects the lives of non-Muslims from assassination just as it protects their bodies from beating and torture. They should not be punished if they are late in fulfilling their obligations, such as paying the *jizyah* and the *kharaj*. Islam does, however, adopt a more serious view toward Muslims who refuse to pay the poor-due (*zakah*).

The *fuqaha'* did not allow severe punishment of those non-Muslims who failed to meet their obligations. Imam Abu Yusuf says: "A companion of the Prophet, Hakim ibn Hisham, saw the ruler of Homs (a city in Syria) punishing some people of Nabatea over their capitation tax. He was shocked: "What is this? I have heard the Prophet, upon whom be peace, saying, 'Verily, Almighty Allah will torture those who torture people in this world.'"[22]

'Ali wrote to the collectors of the *kharaj*:

> When you come to them, do not sell their garments preserved for winter or summer, or the food they eat, or the animals they need. Don't whip any of them for a *dirham*, and do not oblige them to stand on one leg for a *dirham*. Do not sell any of their household goods for the payment of *kharaj*, because we accept from them what they have. If you do not comply with my orders, Allah will punish you in my absence. And if I receive any complaint against you in this concern, your services will be terminated. The officer said, "Then I return to you as I left you."[23]

Protection of Property

Besides protecting the life of a non-Muslim, the Islamic state is bound to

---

[19]Related by Imams At-Tabari and Al-Baihaqi. *As-Sunan Al-Kubra*. Vol. VIII, p. 34.

[20]Abdur Razzaq, *Al-Musannaf*, Vol. X, pp. 101-102.

[21]This is according to Al-Jasas's *Ahkam Al-Qur'an*, Vol. I, Chapter "Qatl Al-Muslim Bi Al-Kubra," pp. 140-144, Istanbul and Beirut.

[22]This was related by Imam Muslim in his *Sahih*. See Abu Yusuf, *Al-Kahraj*, p. 125, and Al-Baihaqi, *As-Sunan Al-Kubra*, Vol. 9, p. 205.

[23]Abu Yusuf, *Al-Kharaj*, pp. 15-16; *As-Sunan Al-Kubra*, Vol. IX, p. 205.

protect his property. All Muslims, regardless of the legal school they follow, have always agreed on this point. Abu Yusuf, in his book *Al-Kharaj*, has quoted the Prophet's contract with the people of Najran:

> Najran and its neighboring area are in the security of Almighty Allah and His Messenger. The property, religions, and churches of the inhabitants, as well as all possessions, whether much or little, are under the protection of the Prophet.[24]

'Umar ibn al-Khattab, in his letter to Abu 'Ubaida ibn al-Jarrah, wrote, "Prevent Muslims from harming or oppressing them (non-Muslims) or from taking their property illegally..." Throughout the ages, Muslims have patterned their attitude toward the non-Muslims on 'Ali's dictum, "They pay the capitation tax so that their blood and wealth may be like ours." Thus, a person who steals from a non-Muslim will have his hand cut off and he who takes their property by violence is punished and obliged to return it to its owner. Also, he who borrows money from a non-Muslim is obliged to repay him; if the borrower is rich and delays payment, he is to be put in prison until he pays his debt.

Islam is so tolerant and indulgent with non-Muslims that it respects what they consider property according to their religion, although it may not be property from the Islamic point of view. For example, someone who destroys wine or pork found in the possession of a Muslim is neither fined nor punished; rather he is rewarded by Allah. A Muslim is not allowed to possess these two items, neither for himself, nor for sale to others. However, the Hanafi *fuquha'* state that if a person finds these two items in the possession of a non-Muslim and destroys them, he must fully compensate the owner.[25]

Protection of Honor

Islam protects the honor of non-Muslims just as it protects the honor of Muslims. Thus, no one may abuse a non-Muslim or bring false charges against him, nor can he be slandered in offensive terms regarding his person, his ancestry, his complexion, physique, character or anything else.

The Maliki scholar Shihab al-Din al-Qarafi has stated in his book, *Al-Furuq,* "The contract of *dhimma* gives them certain rights over us because they are in our land under our protection and under the protection of Almighty Allah, His messenger, and the Islamic religion.[26]

A standard work of the Hanafi school, *Ad-Durr Al-Mukhtar*, states: It is incumbent upon Muslims to abstain from harming non-Muslims. It is forbidden to slander them, just as it is forbidden to slander Muslims. According to 'Allamah Ibn 'Abidin: By virtue of the pact of *dhimma*, they have the same rights which we have. The slander of Muslims is prohibited, as is the slander of non-Muslims.

---

[24] *Al-Kharaj*, p. 72.
[25] Other *fuqaha'* have different opinions.
[26] Vol. II, p. 14 (Farq 119).

It is even said that the sin of annoying a non-Muslim is greater.[27]

Assurance in Case of Disability, Poverty, and Old Age

Islam has ensured a suitable livelihood for all non-Muslims and their families who are subjects of the Islamic state. The Prophet, upon whom be peace, said, "All of you are masters, and every master is responsible for his subjects."[28] This has been practiced since the era of the first four successors of Muhammad, known as the "four rightly-guided caliphs."

The treaty of protection made by Khalid ibn al-Walid with the Christians of Al-Hira in Iraq states:

> Any aged non-Muslim who is unable to earn his livelihood, or is struck by disaster, or who becomes destitute and is helped by the charity of his fellow men will be exempted from the capitation tax and will be supplied with sustenance by the *bait al-mal* (the government treasury).[29]

This decision was made during the reign of Abu Bakr as-Siddique in the presence of a large number of the Prophet's companions. It was written by Khalid ibn al-Walid to Abu Bakr, who did not dispute it. The *fuqaha'*, therefore, consider it as *ijma'*.

'Umar ibn al-Khattab once saw an old Jewish beggar whom he found to be destitute. Ordering the state authorities to pay for his livelihood, he observed, "It is unjust if we collect the capitation tax from him in his youth and abandon him in his old age."[30]

Once when 'Umar was on his way to Syria, he came across some Christian lepers at Jabia. He ordered the financial authorities to give them help from the *zakah* funds and to provide for them.[31]

Islam provides a "social guarantee", as a general principle, which covers all people of the society, Muslim and non-Muslim. It would not be just if a person in a Muslim society were to suffer from hunger, or if he were deprived of clothing, medical treatment, or accommodation. It is incumbent upon a Muslim society to provide for its citizen's needs, regardless of his religion.

In his book, *Al-Minhaj*, Imam An-Nawawi said:

> One of the duties of *fard kifayah* (the Islamic term for collective duty) is that a citizen should be supported if he has no suitable clothes, and that he should be fed if he has no food and is not supported from the poor fund or the government treasury.

---

[27]See *Ad-Durr Al-Mukhtar*, and the notes of Ibn 'Abidin on this issue in Vol. III, pp. 334-346, ed. Istanbul.
[28]Related by Al-Bukhari and Muslim, on the authority of Ibn 'Umar.
[29]*Al-Kharaj*, p. 144.
[30]*Al-Kharaj*, p. 126.
[31]Al-Baladhuri, *Futuh Al-Buldan*, p. 177, ed. Beirut.

'Allama Shams ad-Din ar-Ramli ash-Shafi'i in his book, *Nihaya Al-Muhtaj Ila Sharh Al-Minhaj* makes it clear that non-Muslims are like Muslims in this regard and that their protection from suffering is an obligation upon the Islamic society. He further explains that there are two opinions on this issue: (1) To provide non-Muslims with the means to protect their lives and, (2) To provide suitable provision. As the second is more recognized, they should be given suitable dress and suitable food according to summer and winter seasons, including medicine, treatment, and servant charges. The Muslims should also struggle to free their non-Muslim warriors from prison.

Freedom of Embracing a Religion

Just as it preserves other rights of non-Muslims, Islam also protects their right to embrace a religion of their own choice. One cannot be obliged or compelled to convert to Islam. This is based on Allah's commandment:

"Let there be no compulsion in religion. Truth stands out clear from error." (Al-Baqarah: 256)

Almighty Allah says:

"Will you compel mankind against their will to believe?" (Yunus: 99)

The famous commentator Ibn Kathir has interpreted the meaning of the first *'ayah* (256) as, "Do not compel anyone to embrace Islam as it is self-evident in its proofs and realities and does not need to exert force to be accepted."

This *'ayah*, according to other commentators, was revealed by Allah to indicate the miraculous nature of this religion. It is related by Ibn 'Abbas and his father.

During the jahiliyyah (pre-Islamic times), among other practices the Ansars, out of their animosity toward a tribe, and to avert the possibility of their children following the ways of their enemies, would force their children to become Jews. But, when the Jews of Banu An-Nadhir were being exiled from Madinah, the Ansars got worried about their "Jewish" sons. The preceding *'ayah*[32] was revealed in that context and stood in sharp contrast to the temper of the age marked with forced conversion, intolerance, and persecution. In the then civilized world, the Romans forced their subjects to choose between the state religion and death. They also killed Jacobite Christians and others who did not adhere to the sect chosen by the state. The Qur'an prohibited forced conversion, for when Allah guides a person by opening his heart to the truth, he naturally embraces Islam with full faith and a discerning consciousness. The opposite is also true: when He makes a person's heart blind and seals his eyes and ears, it is useless to attempt to bring about his conversion to Islam by force (as Ibn

---

[32]Ibn Kathir quoted Ibn Jarir as saying, "It is related by Imams Abu Dawood, An-Nisa'i, Ibn Abi Hatim, Ibn Hibban in his *Sahih*, Mujahid, Sa'id ibn Jubair, Ash-Sha'bi, Al-Hasan al-Basri and others say that the *'ayah* was revealed in connection with this situation." See *Tafsir Ibn Kathir*, Vol. I, p. 310.

Kathir explained). Thus, for the Muslim, faith is not the mere recitation of liturgical words, but rather the sincere acceptance, total obedience and submission to its demands. For this reason, there is no historical incident of Muslims forcing any of the non-Muslim citizenry to embrace Islam — a fact acknowledged by western historians as well.

Islam protects the places of worship of non-Muslims, and allows them to observe their religious ceremonies. In addition, it protects their freedom of worship. Allah says:

> To those against whom war is made, permission is given (to fight), because they are wronged — and verily, God is Most Powerful for their aid — (They are) those who have been expelled from their homes in defiance of right, — (for no cause) except that they say, 'Our Lord is God.' Did not God check one set of people by means of another, there surely would have been pulled down monasteries, churches, synagogues, and mosques in which the name of God is (mentioned) in abundant measure. (Al-Hajj: 39-40)

In addition to the covenant made by the Prophet with the Christians of Najran, which placed them under the protection of Allah and his Prophet and provided for the safeguarding of their wealth, religion, and churches, the one made by 'Umar ibn al-Khattab with the citizens of Iliya' (Jerusalem) stated:

> This is the protection which the servant of Allah, 'Umar ibn al-Khattab, the commander of the faithful extends to them (non-Muslims):' The safeguarding of their lives, property, churches, crosses, and of their entire community. Their churches are not to be occupied, demolished, or damaged, nor are their crosses or anything belonging to them to be touched. They will not be forced to abandon their religion, nor will they be harmed. None of the Jews will live with them in Iliya' (Jerusalem)'.[33]

Khalid ibn al-Walid, in his covenant with the people of 'Anat, wrote, "They are allowed to ring their bells at any time of the day or night, except at the Islamic prayer times. They are allowed to bear their crosses in their festivals."[34]

Islam simply wants non-Muslims to consider the feelings of Muslims and respect the sanctity of their religion. Thus, they should not expose their ceremonies or crosses in the Islamic dominions, nor should they erect a church in a city where there had not previously been one, as such an action could provoke anger and thereby lead to disorder and sedition. Some *fuqaha'* were nevertheless tolerant to the point of allowing non-Muslims churches and places of worship in Islamic lands and the conquered territories during the wars against non-Muslims, provided the Muslims' leader felt that it would be in the interests of all concerned. This opinion is quoted from the Zaidiyyah school of thought and

---

[33]*Tarikh At-Tabari*, Vol. III, p. 609, ed. Dar al-Ma'arif, Egypt.
[34]Abu Yusuf, *Al-Kharaj*, p. 146.

from the Maliki Imam Ibn al-Qasim.[35]

Apparently this opinion was adopted in Islamic history right from the beginning. In Egypt, in the first century of the *hijrah*, several churches were constructed, for example, the "Mar Marqas" church of Alexandria was built between 39-56 AH. The first church in the Roman quarter of Fustat (old Cairo) was constructed between 47-68 AH under the rule of Maslama ibn Makhlad. When 'Abdul 'Aziz ibn Marwan established the city of Helwan near Cairo, he allowed the Christians to build a church as well as to establish two monasteries for some bishops. There are several other examples. In his book, *Al-Khitat*, the famous historian Al-Maqrizi has given several examples and concludes, "It is agreed that all the churches of Cairo were established after the coming of Islam."[36] In non-Muslim places and villages, non-Muslims are not forbidden to celebrate their rites openly, to renovate their old churches, or to establish new ones to meet their members' needs. This kind of tolerance toward non-Muslims by a religious people who gained victory and rose to power by their faith is unrecorded elsewhere in the history of religions. This fact is recognized by many western writers. Gustave Lebon says:

> From the said verses of the *Qur'an* we can see that Muhammad's tolerance towards Jews and Christians was truly very great. None of the founders of the religions which appeared before his time, especially Judaism and Christianity, has spoken or acted in this manner. Then we saw how his *caliphs* followed his traditions. This tolerance has been recognized by some European scholars who have deeply contemplated Arab history. The following quotation which I have taken from their numerous books prove that these are not exclusively our opinions. Robertson says in his book *The History of Charles V* that Muslims are the only people who possess both a zeal for their faith as well as a spirit of tolerance toward the followers of other religions. Although they fight for the sake of Islam and its dissemination, they leave those who do not follow their religion free to adhere to their own religious teachings.[37]

Freedom of Work and Profession

Non-Muslims enjoy freedom of work and profession: they may make contracts with others or by themselves, choose any profession, and undertake any kind of economic activity. The *fuqaha'* have ruled that non-Muslims should be treated in the same manner as Muslims in the matters of trade, commerce, and other financial matters, except "riba" (interest), which is forbidden for them as well as for Muslims. It is related that the Prophet, wrote to the Magians of Hajar: "Either abandon *riba* (interest), or be at war with Allah and His messenger."

There are also several other restrictions placed upon them: they are forbidden to sell wines and pork in Muslim lands; they may not open pubs or clubs which

---

[35]See *Ahkam Adh-Dhimmiyyin Wa Al-Musta'minin*, pp. 96-99.
[36]See *Islam and Dhimmis* by Dr. Ali H. Al-Kharbotaly, p. 139.
[37]Lebon, Gustave, *Arab Civilization* (trans. 'Adil Za'aytar), p. 128 (fn).

serve alcoholic drinks; and they may not import these items into Muslim lands in broad daylight, even though it may be for their own entertainment. The intention behind these prohibitions is to prevent any possibility of corruption or disturbance within the Muslim society.

Except for these few restrictions, non-Muslims enjoy full freedom in pursuing their economic and professional interests. Such an assertion can be proved by recorded historical facts; even some professions, such as the exchanging of money, jewelry, and pharmaceutical businesses were their exclusive domains. This was the situation in almost all Muslim countries until recent times. Thus, the non-Muslims accumulated large fortunes from these businesses, for they were exempt from the *zakah* (poor-due) and the *jizyah*, as the latter was only a very small tax levied on those who could afford military service but did not wish to serve.

Adam Mitz writes:

> The Islamic *shari'ah* did not deny the non-Muslims any opportunity to work. They were engaged in lucrative professions; they were money exchangers, traders, jewelers and businessmen, physicians and land-lords. They organized themselves in a lucrative manner. For example, most of the dealers in currency and jewelry in Syria were Jews; and most of physicians, clerks, and scribes were Christians. The Christian leader in Baghdad was the physician of the *caliph*; the Jews' leaders and businessmen were employees of the *caliph*."[38]

Government Services

The non-Muslims have the right to serve in any governmental position which does not have a direct bearing on the religious life of the Muslims. For example, non-Muslims may not serve as *imams* (the head of state), the head of the army, arbiters in inter-Muslim disputes, or as *zakah* collectors. The *imam* and *caliph* are invested with both religious and secular authority, since they are the successors of the Prophet. That is why only a Muslim is authorized to serve in these capacities. Moreover, it is not reasonable to expect a non-Muslim to implement and respect Islamic rules.

The leadership of the army is not a secular post, for Islam regards *jihad* as the greatest act of worship. This also applies to the Islamic judiciary system. As it is rooted in the *shari'ah*, how can a non-Muslim be required to implement rules in which he does not believe? The same is true with the positions of *zakah* collectors and officials entrusted with other posts of religious nature.

Except for these few governmental posts, non-Muslims can be employed in any other capacity, provided they fulfill the necessary requirements of efficiency, trust, and loyalty to the state. As for those who behave with animosity and hatred toward Muslims, Allah has warned:

O You who believe! Do not take into intimacy those outside your ranks.

---

[38]Mitz, Adam, *The Islamic Civilization in the Fourth Century A.H.*, (trans. by Muhammad 'Abdul Hadi Abu Rida), 4th ed., Basle, Switzerland. See the section "Jews and Christians," Vol. I, p. 86.

They will not fail to corrupt you. They only desire your ruin. Rank hatred
has already appeared from their mouths. What their hearts conceive
is far worse. We have made plain to you the signs, if you have wisdom.
(Al-'Imran 118)

Some *fuqaha'* such as Al-Mawardi, are so tolerant that in his notable book
Al-Ahkam As-Sultaniyya, he even allows non-Muslims to have the post of
executive minister, who is responsible for issuing and enforcing the *imam's*
orders. This post is not to be confused with that of the planning minister, to
whom the *imam* entrusts political, administrative, and economic matters at his
own discretion. Some Christians occupied the former post several times during
the 'Abbasid dynasty: Nasr ibn Harun in 369 AH and 'Isa ibn Nasturis in 380
AH. Mu'awiyah, the first 'Umayyad *caliph*, had a Christian named Sarjun as
head office clerk. Muslim governments were sometimes so tolerant that Muslims
would voice their discontent at the unjust preference given to the Jews and
Christians over them.

Writing about the presence of high-ranking non-Muslim government officials,
Adam Mitz observes in his book *Islamic Civilization in the Fourth Century A.H.*,[39]
Christians held highly influential positions in the government. Reports of Muslims' complaints concerning the influence of non-Muslims in the government
had been heard for many years.

An Egyptian poet[40] has expressed the great influence of Jews on the Muslim
rulers of his age, especially by way of their wealth and high-ranking positions:

> The Jews of this age have reached
> the height of their wealth and they possess
> splendor and money,
> among them the advisor and the king.
> O people of Egypt, I advise you
> to become Jews, for the universe has become Jewish.

The last two lines of this poem, quoted by the famous Hanafi *faqih* Ibn 'Abidin,
express his observations on the influence of non-Muslims even in specific legal
and scholastic matters:[41]

> My beloved , nowadays there are many disasters.
> Worst, the fools have become the masters.
> When will time awake from its stupor?
> When will I see the Jews cringe before the *fuqaha'*?

This is, in brief, the impact which Muslim ignorance and deviation from Islam
as well as strong Jewish influence had upon Islamic society during its years of

---

[39]Vol. 1, p. 105.

[40]Al-Hasan ibn Khaqan, as described in As-Suyuti's *Husn Al-Muhadara*, Vol. II, p. 117. See also Adam
Mitz, ibid., Vol. I, p. 118.

[41]Ibn 'Abidin, *Hashiyya Ibn 'Abidin*, Vol. I, p. 379.

decline. During the last years of the Ottoman Empire, many important and sensitive governmental posts were occupied by non-Muslim citizens who in turn appointed Christians as ambassadors and agents abroad. That such appointments compromised the integrity of the empire is a fact of history.

Security for the Fulfillment of These Rights

Although man-made laws and constitutions speak of equal rights and obligations for their citizens, their realization in practice is thwarted because of the prejudices and other tendencies upon which laws can have no impact, and because the people either have no sense of the laws' sacredness or do not believe in submitting to legal authority. Islamic laws are, however, an exception.

Security of Faith

The Islamic shari'ah is the eternal, immutable, and just law of Allah. A Muslim's faith is incomplete without total obedience to it. Allah says:

"It is not fitting for a believer, either man or woman, to have any option about the decision, when a matter has been decided by God and His Apostle." (Al-Ahzab: 26)

Every Muslim who abides by his faith implements its rules and injunctions in order to please his Creator and to earn his reward. Sentiments of relationship or enmity cannot make him deviate from this creed. Allah says:

"O You who believe! Stand out firmly for justice, as witnesses to God, even as against yourselves, or your parents, or your kin." (An-Nisa': 135)

Responsibility of the Islamic Society

An Islamic society is responsible for implementing the shari'ah, even if the issue is of concern to a non-Muslim. Thus, if there are those who do not honestly and effectively perform the said duties or who deviate from the right path, other members of the society should guide them to righteousness by forbidding all bad deeds. They should stand by the oppressed and wronged party regardless of his religion.

Sometimes an incident of injustice may not provoke a complaint from the non-Muslim, but if it does, the Muslim official must listen to him and then deal judiciously with the usurper, regardless of the latter's social standing. A non-Muslim is, therefore, entitled to file his complaint with the governor of a province or a local official. If his case does not receive due consideration, he may complain to a higher authority, or even to the caliph, until he is satisfied that justice has been done. If he were to challenge the caliph himself, his case would be presided over by an autonomous body authorized to sentence the head of state.

In addition to this, there is the guarantee offered by the widespread general Islamic conscience instilled in Muslims by the Islamic creed and traditions.

History has recorded outstanding examples of this, two of which will suffice to illustrate the point. A Christian monk in Egypt lodged a complaint with the ruler Ahmad ibn Tulun against one of his military leaders who had illegally taken some money from him. The ruler summoned the leader to his office and after admonishing him, took the money from him and gave it to the monk. Then the ruler told the monk, "If you had claimed more money, I would have got it returned back to you, too." By this act of justice, the ruler opened the doors for any oppressed non-Muslim to regain his rights, even though the accused might be a high ranking military or government official. If the governor or his relatives are the source of the oppression, the *imam* or the *caliph* should intervene and stop it.

The other example is the well-known story of a Copt and 'Amr ibn al-'As, the ruler of Egypt. The ruler's son, proud of his parentage, hit the Copt's son with a whip. The Copt complained to 'Umar ibn al-Khattab, who then summoned 'Amr and his son to Madinah. 'Umar gave the whip to the Copt's son and said, "Whip this son of noble parents." After he had done so, 'Umar said, "Now whip the bald head of 'Amr, because his son beat you on account of his father's authority." The Copt replied, "I have already whipped the person who whipped me." Then 'Umar turned his face to 'Amr and uttered his everlasting words, "O 'Amr, since when do you treat as slaves those who were born as free men?" What is most remarkable about this incident is the fact that people ruled by Islamic officials were so aware of their humanity and honor that even a slap was totally inadmissible. On the other hand, in Roman and other times, many similar and even worse injustices went unpunished, for the injured party could not make any protest or complaint. In the Islamic state, however, a citizen could take advantage of his rights and self respect, even if he had to travel from Egypt to Madinah to do so. Such a journey would not be in vain, for he could be sure that his case would be given due consideration and that his complaint would be dealt with justly.

If a non-Muslim could not approach a *caliph*, or if the latter's behavior was like that of the local governor in the non-Muslim's home province, he could then try to rouse public opinion, represented by the *fuqaha'* and all pious Muslims, so as to gain support for his cause. An outstanding example of this is Imam Al-Awza'i's attitude toward an 'Abbasid ruler who had exiled one of the non-Muslim tribes from Mount Lebanon after some of them had refused to cooperate with the *kharaj* collector. The ruler, Salih ibn 'Ali ibn 'Abdullah ibn 'Abbas, was a relative of the *caliph*. Al-Awza'i wrote him a detailed letter in which he stated:

> How can all of these people be punished and driven from their lands and properties because of some individual transgressors? Allah states (in Surah An-Najm 38): '... no bearer of burdens can bear the burden of another.' This is the true ordinance to be followed. The Prophet, gave the following advice which is well worth practicing: If any man oppresses a non-Muslim or tries him beyond his strength, I will advocate for the oppressed. (Al-Awza'i further stated) ...They (that is, the *dhimmis*) are not slaves to be transferred from place to place, but they

are free men and *ahl adh-dhimma*.[42]

Islamic history abounds with such cases. Whenever a usurpation of the non-Muslims' rights took place, the fuqaha' and public opinion put their weight behind them in the restitution of their rights.

One of the Umayyad *caliphs*, Al-Walid ibn 'Abdul Malik, appropriated the Church of Saint John from the local Christians and had it incorporated into the mosque. When 'Umar ibn 'Abdul 'Aziz became *caliph*, the Christians complained to him about this matter. 'Umar wrote to his governor, instructing him to return the annexed church to the Christians if a suitable agreement concerning compensation could not be reached.[43]

During his reign, Al-Walid ibn Yazid, exiled all non-Muslims from Cyprus and sent them to Syria. This was done as a precautionary measure, for he feared a siege by the Romans. However, the *fuqaha'* and the public were angered by this action and considered such a decision to be unjust. When his son Yazid Ibn al-Walid came to power, he let the non-Muslims return to Cyprus. His attitude was appreciated and considered by Muslims as a just action. The historian Al-Baladhuri mentions this incident as one of his virtues. [44]

The Islamic system grants its judiciary great power and autonomy. Every citizen, regardless of his religion or genealogy, can seek the restitution of his rights against any person, no matter how powerful.

There are several examples of Islamic justice in which the *caliph* had to appear in court, either as a defendant or a petitioner, and was compelled to accept the judgment. We would like to quote one example pertinent to our subject:

'Ali once lost his coat of mail and later found it in the possession of a Christian. They took the matter to the judge Shuraih. 'Ali stated, 'This is my coat of mail which I neither sold nor gave away.' The judge turned to the Christian and asked what he had to say against the complainant. The Christian answered, "This coat of mail belongs to

---

[42]See Al-Baladhuri, *Futuh Al-Buldan*, p. 222, and Abu 'Ubaid, *Al-Amwal*, pp. 170-171.

[43]The story of the Church of Saint John, as related by Al-Baladhuri, is as follows: Since the time of Mu'awiyah, all of the *caliphs* up to 'Abdul Malik had tried to obtain this church from the Christians so that the premises of the Umayyad Mosque could be extended. The Christians, however, refused. During the reign of Al-Walid, they were offered a considerable sum of money as compensation for the church, but again they refused, whereupon he said to them, "If you do not agree, I will tear this church down." Some of them replied, "O Prince of the Faithful, he who tears down a church will be afflicted with madness or curse." This utterance angered him so much that he asked for a pickax and began to demolish the church walls with his own hands. He then ordered some laborers to demolish it completely, and the space was subsequently annexed to the mosque. When 'Umar ibn 'Abdul 'Aziz was elected *caliph*, the Christians complained to him. He ordered that the space be restored to them. The people of Damascus, however, did not agree with this decision, and objected in the following terms, "How can we demolish our mosque after having prayed there?" Sulaiman ibn Habib al-Muharibi and other *fuqaha'* attempted to satisfy the Christians by suggesting that they be given all the churches of Ghutah (in the suburbs of Damascus) which, having been conquered by force, was now the property of the Islamic state. The Christians willingly accepted this offer as just compensation for the Church of Saint John. The Muslims wrote to 'Umar, who was pleased with this settlement.

[44]Ibid., p. 214.

none other than myself, but I do not call the Prince of the Faithful a liar." Then turning to 'Ali again the judge asked him for his witnesses. 'Ali was unable to provide any, and smiled, saying, "Shuraih is right, I have no witnesses." The judge thus accorded the coat of mail to the Christian since it was in his possession and because 'Ali had no witnesses to prove his ownership. The man then took it and went his way. But he had not gone too far when he returned, saying, "These are indeed the laws of the prophets! The Prince of the Faithful presented this case to the judge who decided in my favor. I bear witness that there is no god but Allah and that Muhammad is His Prophet! This is your coat of mail, O Prince of the Faithful. I was following your army as you were returning from the battle of Siffin. Your coat of mail fell from your camel." 'Ali answered, "Since you have embraced Islam, this coat of mail is yours!"[45]

This is a true event which needs no further comment.

---

[45]Ibn Kathir, *Al-Bidaya Wa An-Nihaya*, Vol. VIII, pp. 4-5.

II / Obligations Of The Ahl Adh-Dhimma

Having dealt with the rights of the non-Muslim citizens in an Islamic society, and the guarantees for the protection and implementation of those rights, we will now discuss their obligations, since every right has a corresponding obligation.

These obligations are:

To pay the *jizyah*, the *kharaj*, and the commercial tax, that is, monetary obligations.

To abide by Islamic laws in civil matters and so forth.

To respect Islamic ceremonies, places of worship, and feelings.

Jizyah and Kharaj

The *jizyah* and *kharaj* are small per capita annual obligations levied on adults who can financially afford it — the poor are totally exempted. Allah says:

"God puts no burden on any person beyond what he has given him." (At-Talaq: 7)

The *jizyah* has no fixed limit; it is left to the discretion of the *imam* to decide how much each individual should pay. 'Umar ibn al-Khattab fixed the *jizyah* at 48 *dirhams* for the wealthy, 24 *dirhams* for the middle class and 12 *dirhams* for those who did not fit in the first two categories. He was thus the first person to introduce the principle of taxation according to financial means, an idea which has many supporters today.

We find that there is no inconsistency between his action and that of the Prophet when he sent Mu'adh ibn Jabal as his deputy to Yemen. He advised him to take only one *dinar* from every adult,[1] as they were very poor.

The *jizyah* (capitation) tax is justified by a verse from the *Qur'an*:

Fight those who believe not in God nor the Last Day, nor hold forbidden that which has been forbidden by God and the Apostle, nor acknowledge the religion of Truth (even if they are) of the *people of the book*, until they pay the *jizyah* with willing submission, and feel themselves

---

[1] Related by Imam Ahmad and others whose hadith compilations make up the *Sunan*. It has also been related as a sound *hadith* by Imam At-Tirmidhi.

subdued. (At-Tawbah: 29)

This implies willing submission, disarmament, and total capitulation and obedience to the constitution of the state. The Prophet, upon whom be peace, levied the *jizyah* upon the Magians of Bahrain. The first four caliphs (*al-khulafa' ar-rashidun*) also levied *jizyah* on the *people of the book* and all those in the conquered territories who fell into this category.

The *kharaj* is a property tax levied on land owned by a non-Muslim. The assessment of this tax is left to the *imam's* judgment. He is authorized to fix the ratio of the land's yield, such as one-third or one-fourth, or to fix a specific quantity in weight or measure according to its agricultural yield. ('Umar ibn al-Khattab choose this latter method in dealing with the lands of Iraq.) It may also be a determined sum of money. The difference between the *jizyah* and the *kharaj* is that the former is cancelled after a non-Muslim embraces Islam, while the latter must still be paid, meaning that a non-Muslim would continue to pay it even after he had embraced Islam. The new convert to Islam is also required to give one-tenth or one-twentieth of his land's yield, in addition to the *kharaj* levied on his land. This is the opinion of the three imams of the Islamic legal (*fiqhi*) schools. The fourth, Imam Abu Hanifah, has a different opinion. Many *fuqaha'* agree with him. This tax is therefore similar to the present-day property tax, whereas the *'ushr* (tithe) is similar to the agricultural yield or production tax.

Why Dhimmis are Obliged to Pay the Jizyah

Some people, looking at this issue superficially, think that the imposition of the *jizyah* on non-Muslims by Islam is unfair. But if they were to consider the matter logically, they would realize that Islam was very just in this matter.

Islam obliges all Muslims to perform military service as an individual or a collective duty (*fard 'am* or *fard kifayah*) to protect the state. At the same time, Islam exempts non-Muslims from this duty, though they live in the state. The reason behind this practice is that the Islamic state, since it is based on a specific doctrine and ideology, is best protected by those who believe in it. It is not reasonable to expect a person who does not believe in the ideology of his country to sacrifice his life for the sake of its protection, or for the sake of a religion in which he does not believe. That is why Islam imposes *jihad* only on Muslims. It is a sacred religious duty and an act of worship which brings Muslims closer to Allah. It has been stated that the divine reward for *jihad* is greater than that of the believer who fasts and prays.

Islam does, however, expect non-Muslim citizens to contribute to the expenses of the state's defense and protection by means of the *jizyah*. Thus, besides being a sign of obedience to the Islamic government, the *jizyah* is, in fact, a financial substitute for the military service imposed on every Muslim adult who is able and fit for combat. It is not imposed on women or minors, since they are not allowed to fight. 'Umar ibn al-Khattab said to one of his collectors, "Do not impose it on women or minors." This is why the *fuqaha'* state: "If a woman pays the *jizyah* for residency in the Islamic state, she is allowed residency for free and the sum must be returned to her, since it is not imposed on women. If she knows that it is not imposed on women and nonetheless gives the sum willingly, then it is accepted from her as a gift." Into this category fall the aged, the blind, the disabled, and the mentally impaired, as well as those who are unable to perform military service. The Muslims were so tolerant that they even exempted monks from this tax. The rational being that since they had dedicated their lives to worship in their churches, they could not be enrolled into the military.[2]

The historian Adam Mitz is of the view that because of Islamic tolerance toward non-Muslims and by virtue of the protection granted to them, they paid the *jizyah* in accordance with their financial capacities. This *jizyah* was like the present-day national defense tax. Only persons who could perform military service were obliged to pay it. So Monks and ascetics were exempted, except for those who could afford to pay.[3] Another reason for placing this tax on non-Muslims is similar to that used by governments of any age to justify their taxes. All citizens should pay some of the expenses for public services established for the common good, such as courts, police, public works, repairing of roads and bridges, as well as all other services which lead to the enjoyment of a normal life for all. Muslims support these by paying their *zakah*, *sadaqat al-fitr*, and other alms. It is therefore not surprising that a minimal tax, such as the *jizyah*, should be levied on non-Muslims. The regulations concerning this tax are spelled out by the Maliki school of thought.[4]

When is the Jizyah not Applied?

As has already been explained, this tax assures non-Muslims the protection of the Islamic state. Should the state become unable to provide this protection, it may not collect this tax. This rule was followed by Abu 'Ubaidah when he learned of the situation in several Syrian cities. Syria had fallen into the hands of the Muslims, but as the Romans were gathering troops to regain it, he decided not to undertake the protection of the non-Muslims. The *jizyah* was, therefore, returned with the announcement:

> We have returned your money to you because we have been informed of the gathering of enemy troops. You people, according to the conditions stipulated in the contract, have obliged us to protect you. Since we are now unable to fulfill these conditions, we are returning your money to you. We will abide by the conditions as agreed upon if we overcome the enemy.[5]

Similar conditions were laid in several treaties concluded between the Muslim

---

[2]*Ula* An-Nuha. Vol. II, p. 96.
[3]*Islamic Civilization*, Vol. I, p. 96.
[4]See the *Risala* of Ibn Abi Zaid and the two commentaries upon it by Ibn Naji and Zaruqi, Vol. I, p. 331 ff.
[5]Related by Abu Yusuf in *Al-Kharaj*.

commanders and the non-Muslims, including the one by Khalid ibn al-Walid: "If we are able to protect you, we have the right to your *jizyah*, otherwise we do not, until we overcome the enemy," as stated in At-Tabari's history. The obligation of paying this tax is also cancelled when non-Muslims participate with Muslims in defending the Islamic state against its enemies. Such conditions were clearly stated in contracts and other documents signed by Muslims and non-Muslims during the reign of 'Umar ibn al-Khattab .[6]

As to the *jizyah's* collection and the dates upon which it fell due, the author of *Islam Wa Ahl Adh-Dhimma* reported[7] that it was collected once every lunar year.[8] It could also be paid in cash or in goods except carrion or swine. 'Umar ibn al-Khattab decreed that payment of this tax be made as easy as possible by saying: "Accept whatever is possible from those who are unable to pay the *jizyah* and help those who have become incapable, since we do not want (it from) them for a year or two."[9] The Islamic state, as reported by Abu 'Ubaid, would often postpone collecting this tax until the harvesting season, so that the non-Muslims were able to pay it without being inconvenienced by it in any way.[10]

The Islamic state treated its non-Muslim citizens with kindness and compassion while collecting the *jizyah*. Once, during the reign of 'Umar ibn al-Khattab, a *jizyah* collector offered the taxes collected from the people to 'Umar, who was upset by the large amount and asked him if he had burdened the people. He replied, "No, not at all! We took only the surplus and lawful taxes." 'Umar asked, "Without any pressure or persecution?" The man replied, "Yes." 'Umar then said to him, "Praise be to Almighty Allah that the non-Muslim citizens have not been oppressed during my rule."[11]

Commercial Tax

'Umar ibn al-Khattab imposed this tax on the *dhimmis*, each year when they left one region for another, at the rate of one-twentieth of their commercial capital. This is equivalent to the customs duty of our times. Anas ibn Malik and Ziyad ibn Hudair have reported that 'Umar used to take one-fortieth from Muslim merchants, one twentieth from non-Muslim merchants, and one-tenth from the merchants of *ahl al-harb*, meaning those who came from a region at war with the Muslims.[12]

The percentage imposed upon Muslim merchants equals the amount of *zakah* they are required to pay on their inventory, whether they travel or not. This is

---

[6]See Zaidan, 'Abdul Karim, *Ahkam Adh-Dhimmiyin Wa Al-Must'minin Fi Dar Al-Islam,* p. 155 ff, and Al-Baladhuri, *Futuh Al-Buldan,* (ed. Beirut), p. 217, where it is stated that the emissary of Abu 'Ubaida made a compromise with a party of the Christian Jarajima: if they would support the Muslims and keep an eye on their enemies, they would not have to pay the *jizyah*.
[7]*Islam Wa Ahl Adh-Dhimma,* pp. 70-71.
[8]*Al-Ahkam As-Sultaniya,* p. 138.
[9]Ibn 'Asakir, *History of Damascus,* Vol. I, p. 178.
[10]*Al-Amwal,* p. 44.
[11]Ibn Salam, Imam Abu 'Ubayd al-Qasim, *Al-Amwal,* Dar Ash-Sharq, Cairo, p. 43.
[12]*Ibid.,* pp. 710-712.

a clear-cut matter. The percentage imposed on merchants of *ahl al-harb* is equal to the percentage they impose on Muslim merchants. Ziyad ibn Hudair was once asked, "From whom did you take the tithe?" He replied, "We did not take the tithe from Muslims or non-Muslims. We took it only from the merchants of *ahl al-harb*, just as they take it only from our (Muslim) merchants."[13] Thus 'Umar's policy, as described by Abu 'Ubaid, was apparent in both instances.[14]

The *fuqaha'* have offered different explanations for the non-Muslim merchants being required to pay an amount equal to one-twentieth the value of their commodities as a tax. Imam Abu 'Ubaid said that the quantity depended on the conditions stipulated between the non-Muslim merchants and 'Umar ibn al-Khattab: "In the case of *dhimmi* merchants, I initially thought that since they were not Muslims, one-fortieth could not be taken from them, and since they were not from *ahl al-harb* who take the tithe from us (Muslims), they could not pay the tithe. I, therefore, examined the matter and finally came across the information that 'Umar had come to terms with them on such and such a quantity in addition to *jizyah* and *kharaj*." Abu 'Ubaid concluded: "I think that 'Umar took (the said quantity) from their merchants according to the terms of the agreement. Thus it became a right of the Muslims over them."[15]

Imam Ibn Shihab az-Zuhri, a famous *tabi'* and *faqih*, put it in another way. As narrated by Ishaq ibn Isa, Anas asked Az-Zuhri, "...why did 'Umar take the tithe from the non-Muslims? He replied that they had paid the same amount since pre-Islamic times, so 'Umar decided to institute it." Abu 'Ubaid preferred the first reason, which was more typical of 'Umar. This was also the opinion of Imam Malik.[16]

Some Hanafi *'ulema* claimed that the tax on non-Muslims was levied for their protection. This would be reasonable, for non-Muslim merchants were in greater need of protection than Muslim merchants, since thieves were more greedy for the property of non-Muslims than for that of Muslims.[17]

Abul A'la al-Maududi thinks that at that time it was mainly the Muslims who formed the defense forces of their Islamic state, while commerce was run by the non-Muslims. To safeguard the commercial interests of the Muslim community, the *fuqaha'* thought it wise to reduce the tax on Muslim merchants so that they could be encouraged toward trade and industry.[18]

But since it is a known fact that the *fuqaha'* based their opinion on 'Umar's action, it would only be right to attribute this taxation to him and not to the *fuqaha'*. As to the taxation and its effect on the Muslim merchants, it would have benefited them only if their taxes had been decreased. But it did not happen that way. He raised the taxes on the non-Muslim merchants without decreasing the taxes on their Muslim counterparts. If Al-Maududi's argument is accepted, than one can presume that since the taxes on the non-Muslims

---

[13]*Ibid.*, p. 706.
[14]*Ibid.*, p. 709.
[15]*Ibid.*, pp. 709-710.
[16]*Ibid.*, p. 713.
[17]*Sharh al-'Inaya 'Ala al-Hidaya*, Vol. I, p. 532.
[18]Al-Maududi, Abul A'la, *Rights of Dhimmis in the Islamic State*, (ed. Dar al-Fikr), p. 25.

were less than the taxes on the Muslim merchants, 'Umar tried to remove this anomaly by raising them on the formers. This is in consonance with 'Umar's character because he was just and God-fearing.

These various justifications are referred to because there is no authentic text dealing with this matter. There is 'Umar's action, which he followed on his own and out of consideration for the common interest of Muslims as outlined in the *shari'ah*. Even if we were to accept the opinion of Abu 'Ubaid that the percentage was a result of 'Umar's agreement with the non-Muslims, we maintain that the items of an agreement are always based on common interest and immediate considerations, which may change later. I prefer Dr. 'Abdul Karim Zaidan's opinion, that the percentage was doubled because non-Muslims are obliged to pay taxes only on that property which they use while trading from one region to another. Any interior capital, (gold, silver, crops, livestock and so on) is not taxable, whereas Muslims are obliged to pay *zakah* on any property belonging to them. Thus, Muslims have greater financial obligations than non-Muslims. It would, therefore, be impossible to make the tax on Muslims equal to that levied on non-Muslims. The reason is that whatever is taken from a Muslim is considered as *zakah*, meaning that its percentage has been fixed and cannot be altered, for it is a form of compulsory worship. It could be argued that a non-Muslim pays the *jizyah* as well as the *kharaj* and that his obligations come close to a Muslim's. However, we could reply by saying that the latter tax is not levied exclusively on a non-Muslim after he embraces Islam, for Muslims are also obliged to pay it if they possess taxable lands. As to the *jizyah*, which is levied only on non-Muslims, it is a very small amount and is not levied on those non-Muslims who are fit for military service. If for some reason the non-Muslims are obliged to pay taxes on all of their public and private property (cattle, agricultural produce, money,and merchandise), it will be proportionately equal to the *zakah* paid by Muslims. In such a case, there would be no reason for grievance, since both the Muslim and the non-Muslim merchants would then be paying equal taxes.

Abiding by the Islamic Constitution

Both Muslims and non-Muslims are obliged to abide by the Islamic constitution since, according to the contract, they are members of the Islamic state. As this constitution does not interfere with their religious freedom, they are not required to fulfill any Islamic religious duties or any other duties of a religious or ritualistic nature, such as paying the *zakah*, or participating in a *jihad*. They are not obliged, in either their personal or social affairs, to abstain from anything which is lawful in their religion but which may be unlawful in Islam, such as marriage and divorce practices, or consuming pork and wine. Islam allows them what they believe to be lawful and does not threaten them with exile or censure. For example, if a Magian marries one of his close relatives (such as his sister, mother, daughter and so on) or a Jew marries his niece, or a Christian eats pork or drinks wine, Islamic laws are not applied to them. Muslims are ordered to leave them to their beliefs. If, of their own volition, they wish to bring their cases to the Islamic courts, these will be decided according to the *shari'ah*.

Allah says:

> "So judge between them by what God has revealed and follow not their vain desires." (Al-Ma'idah: 51)

Some *fuqaha'* have said that it is up to the Muslims to decide whether or not non-Muslim disputes should be settled according to the *shari'ah*. An Islamic court may choose not to hear these cases if it does not want to get involved.

> "If they do come to you, either judge between them, or decline to interfere. If you decline, they cannot hurt you in the least. If you judge, judge in equity before them, for God loves those who judge in equity." (Al-Ma'idah: 45)

It is up to them to decide whether to litigate in their traditional courts or in the Islamic courts. Adam Mitz finds many such instances in Islamic history. Elaborating upon this point, he says that since the Islamic *shari'ah* was intended for Muslims, the Islamic state let non-Muslims settle their disputes in their own courts. Bounded by the *shari'ah*, the Islamic state did not interfere with the jurisdiction of these courts which adjudicated upon matrimony, succession and the related issues among the Christians.

The courts, according to him, were presided by capable judges who wrote commentaries on the law. "So great was the freedom, "he says, "that those who wished to petition their cases in Islamic courts were not looked upon favorably." To discourage Christians' resort to the Islamic courts, and to fill the need for Christian laws, Jathlin Taymonous wrote a book on the subject in 200 AH / 800 AD. Adam Mitz also cites Khair ibn Na'im who in 120 AH / 738 AD took charge of Egypt's courts. He used to carry out his judicial duties on the mosque premises for Muslims, and in the afternoon, he would meet the Christians outside the mosque. Afterwards, judges fixed a day at their houses during which Christians could come and settle their cases. In 177 AH, Qadi Muhammad ibn Masruq took charge of Egypt's judiciary. He was the first judge who allowed the Christians to come into the mosque to settle their cases ... Mitz says that in Andalucia the Christians settled their disputes by themselves, and that they did not resort to the *qadi* except in cases of murder.

Non-Muslims are also required to abide by the Islamic constitution in cases of murder, wealth, honor, civil and criminal affairs, selling and so forth, just like Muslims. In this regard, the *fuqaha'* have said: "They have the rights which we have, and the obligations which we have." Thus, if a non-Muslim is found guilty of stealing, he would be punished exactly as a Muslim culprit would be, and if a non-Muslim kills a person, steals or violates somebody's property, fornicates or accuses a woman of committing fornication, or commits similar crimes, he would be treated like a Muslim culprit, for he has agreed to abide by the Islamic constitution in matters which do not contradict his religion.

Imam Abu Hanifah is of the opinion that both male and female non-Muslims who have been found guilty of adultery should be punished with lashes and not with death by stoning. He bases this opinion on his belief that capital punishment in this case requires that the accused be a Muslim. Civil and financial cases, such as selling, buying, hiring, sharing companies, mortgages, pre-emption, peasantry, reviving barren lands, drafts, guarantees and other contracts and exercises which are the medium of wealth, benefits and means of livelihood are to be dealt with in a similar manner. Thus, all bargaining and contracts which are lawful for Muslims are also lawful for non-Muslims. The reverse is also true, except in the cases of wine and pork. Several *fuqaha'* have excluded these two items, since the Christians believe in their lawfulness. However, they are required to act discreetly in these matters. The charging of interest by non-Muslims is also prohibited, as their own religions also prohibit it.

Consideration for the Feelings of Muslims

The third obligation placed upon non-Muslims is that they should respect the feelings of the surrounding Muslims and the dignity of the Islamic state which takes care of and protects them. They are therefore not allowed to publicly abuse Islam, its messenger, or the *Qur'an*. They may not propagate faiths and creeds contrary to the ideology and religion of the state, provided that these are not parts of their faith, such as the doctrines of the Trinity and the Crucifixion held by the Christians.

They are not allowed to openly indulge in consumption of wine, pork or other items prohibited in Islam, just as they are not allowed to sell those prohibited items to Muslims. They should not take their meals openly during Ramadan, in deference to the feelings of fasting Muslims.

If they engage in practices which are forbidden in Islam but are quite legal according to the teachings of their religions, they are forbidden to announce it openly or to do it in a way which may constitute a challenge to Islamic beliefs and practices. Such matters should be handled properly so that all parts of the society may be in harmony and in peace with each other.

'Arafa ibn al-Harith, a companion of the Prophet, participated with 'Ikrimah in negotiations for peace in Yemen. 'Arafa called upon a Christian to embrace Islam, instead he abused the Prophet. 'Arafa brought the case to 'Amr ibn al-'As[19]:

"God forbid! How can we conclude a pact with them when they mock us regarding our Creator and His Messenger? No, we concluded a treaty with them to leave them and their churches and beliefs in peace; that we would not oppress them, but rather that we would protect them, running the risk of war for their sake. We promised not to interfere in their disputes unless they willingly brought their matters before our

---

[19]Related by Imam At-Tabarani through a line of transmission from 'Abdullah ibn Salih, the author of *Al-Laith*. 'Abdul Malik ibn Sa'id states that this 'Abdullah was a trustworthy and reliable person, but one group of scholars has claimed that he was not trustworthy. The remainder of the transmission chain is trustworthy. See *Majma' Az-Zawa'id*, Vol. 6, p. 13.

before our courts, in which case we would arbitrate according to our *shari'ah*.

"'Amr replied, 'Yes, you are quite correct.'"

III / A Unique Tolerance

Degrees of Tolerance and Behavior of Muslims

There are degrees to religious tolerance. The lowest degree is that of allowing one's opponent to enjoy the freedom of his faith. Doubtless in such a case, the individual is allowed to enjoy freedom of faith, but he might not be able to exercise his religious obligations or to abstain from prohibitions according to his faith.

A moderate degree of tolerace is to allow an individual to believe in a faith of his choice. In this case, he is neither compelled to discard his religious obligations nor is he forced to act contrary to his faith. For instance, a Jew believes that working on Saturdays is prohibited in his faith. Forcing him to work on that day is, therefore, not tolerance [1]. Likewise a Christian, who goes to church on Sundays as part of his faith, should not be constrained from attending it.

The highest degree of tolerance is allowing people of other faiths to follow their way, even though some of their practices might conflict with the religion of the majority. It was this degree of tolerance that the Muslims adopted toward their non-Muslim citizens.

Muslims tolerated the religious practices of their minorities by not prohibiting even those practices which were contrary to the state ideology. Such prohibitions, if Muslims had imposed them on non-Muslims, would not have been considered as fanaticism, for that which is considered lawful in a religion is not necessarily an imposed obligation. For example, although a Magian may marry his mother or sister, he may also marry any other woman without this being frowned upon; or a Christian, who is permitted to eat pork, may also eat beef or lamb or poultry, just as he may abstain from drinking wine, even though the Gospels permit the consumption of wine. Consequently, had Islam ordered the non-Muslims to abstain from marriage with close relatives, which is prohibited by the *shari'ah*, or to abstain from wine or pork for the sake of their Muslim brothers, this would not have caused them any religious conflicts, since these practices are not obligatory for them. Nevertheless, Islam did not make any such demands, nor did it ever intend to take non-Muslims to task on matters

---

[1] It is stated in the Hanbali *Ghayat* Al-Muntaha and its commentary: "To compel a Jew to work on Saturday is prohibited. This order is valid in his case because he is not obliged to work on his Sabbath day, according to the *shari'ah*. A *hadith* related by Imam Nasa'i and authenticated by At-Tirmidhi states: "And you Jews especially should not commit any offense on Saturdays. "

lawful in their religion but unlawful in Islam. On the contrary, Islam enjoins upon Muslims to allow non-Muslims to observe any practice which they believe to be lawful in their religion.

The Muslim Tolerance

There is another aspect of this matter which cannot be found in the edicts of the law, nor can it be enforced by the courts or the government: this is the so-called "spirit of tolerance" which underlies upright attitudes, benevolent dealings, respect for one's neighbors, and all the sincere sentiments of piety, compassion, and courtesy. Such attitudes are required in everyday life and cannot be obtained through constitutional legislation or the courts' jurisdiction. The spirit of tolerance is exclusively practiced in Islamic society. It appears in several verses of the *Qur'an*, which tell of parents who attempted to turn their sons from the unicity of God to polytheism:

"You bear them company in this life with justice." (Luqman: 15)

Similar too is the call of the *Qur'an* to righteousness and justice in dealings with the non-Muslims who do not oppose Muslims in their religion:

"God forbids you not, with regard to those who fight you not for (your) faith nor drive you out of your homes, from dealing kindly and justly with them, for God loves those who are just." (Al-Mumtahanah: 8)

The *Qur'an* describes the righteous in the following terms:

"And they feed, for the love of God, the indigent, the orphan, and the captive." (Al-Insan: 8)

The captives, at the time of this verse's revelation, were polytheists. The *Qur'an* also explains that there is no harm in incurring expenses on behalf of polytheists who are relatives or neighbors of Muslims:

"It is not required of you (O Apostle) to set them on the right path, but God sets on the right path whom He pleases. Whatever good you give benefits your own souls. And you shall only do so seeking the "Face of God ." (Al-Baqarah: 272)

Muhammad ibn al-Hasan, Abu Hanifah's colleague and scribe, has reported that the Prophet had sent money to the people of Makkah when they were facing drought. It was to be distributed among the poor, although the Prophet and his companions had undergone a great deal of torture and oppression at the Makkan's hands.[2] Imams Al-Bukhari, Muslim,and Ahmad related on the

---

[2] *Sharh As-Siyar Al-Kabir*, Vol. I, p. 144.

authority of 'Asma bint Abi Bakr that she said:

"During the covenant with the Quraish, my polytheistic mother came to see me. I asked the Prophet, upon whom be peace, 'O Messenger of Allah, if my mother came to me wishing to see me, should I maintain good relations with her?' He replied, 'Yes, you should treat her kindly.'"[3]

The words of the *Qur'an* indicate the correct manner of discussion with non-Muslims:

And do not dispute with the *people of the book*, except with means better (than mere disputation), unless it be with those of them who inflict wrong (and injury). But say: 'We believe in the Revelation which has come down to us and in that which came down to you. Our God and your God is one.'" (Al-Ankabut: 46)

This tolerance manifests itself very clearly in the conduct of the Prophet, in his dealings with the *people of the book*, whether Christians or Jews. The Prophet used to visit them, treat them kindly and with respect, console their sick, and deal with them in terms of "live and let live."

Ibn Ishaq in his *Sirah* (biography of the Prophet) stated:

When the delegation of Najrani Christians came to the Prophet at Madinah, they entered his mosque in the afternoon to meet him. It was their prayer time, so they began to perform their prayer in the mosque. Some Muslims were about to prevent them from doing so, but the Prophet, upon whom be peace, said, 'Let them pray.' So they faced eastward and performed their prayer.

Based on the preceding incident, Ibn al-Qayyim, a *mujtahid* scholar, put up a sign in front of the mosque reading "*Admission granted to people of the book.*[4] That the people of the book could perform their prayers in the presence of Muslims was evidently clear to him.

In his *Al-Amwal*, Abu 'Ubaid related, on the authority of Sa'id ibn Al-Musayyeb, that the Prophet gave some charity to a Jewish family, which was still being paid to them without interruption.[5] Imam Al-Bukhari related, on the authority of Anas, that the Prophet visited an ailing Jew and called him to Islam. The Jew embraced Islam, and the Prophet left the house praising Allah that, by means of His Prophet's teachings, He had saved the Jew from the fire of Hell.

Imam Al-Bukhari also reports that the Prophet borrowed some money from a Jew. The Jew took the Prophet's coat of mail as security. When the Prophet died, it was still in the Jew's possession. The Prophet could have borrowed money from his companions, but he wanted to teach his *ummah* how to behave

---

[3] *Tafsir Ibn Kathir*, Vol. 9. p. 349.
[4] Zad Al-Ma'ad, Vol. III, As-Sunnah Al-Muhammadiyya Press.
[5] Al-Amwal, p. 613.

toward other people. The Prophet accepted gifts from non-Muslims. He also accepted their assistance in times of war and peace since he was pleased with their friendship and did not fear plots or malevolence on their part.

Once, he stood up when he saw a funeral procession pass. His companions said, "That is the dead body of a Jew." He replied, "Is it not a human soul?!"

This tolerance toward non-Muslims appeared also in the behavior of the Prophet's companions and in their followers of the next generation (the *tabi'n*).

'Umar ibn al-Khattab conferred a permanent salary upon a Jew and his family from the state treasury, quoting the words of Allah:

"Alms are for the poor and the needy ..." (At-Tawbah: 60)

He then added, "This man is one of the indigents of the *people of the book*."[6]

Once, on his way to Syria, 'Umar came across a group of Christian lepers. Taking pity on them, he ordered a social assistance to be paid to them from the state treasury.

'Umar's assassin was one Abu Lu'lu', a Magian non-Muslim. Even though he was on his death-bed as a result of the Magian's assassination attempt on him, he gave instructions to his successor to be merciful to non-Muslims: "I advise the *caliph* who will succeed me to be kind to the non-Muslims, to fulfill our covenant with them, to fight for the sake of their protection, and not to overburden them ..."[7]

Ibn 'Umar used to advise his servant to give his neighbor a portion of the *udhiya* meat (sacrificed animal). He reiterated his concern so much that the servant finally asked him about the secrecy behind such concern toward that neighbor who was a Jew. Ibn 'Umar explained, "The Prophet said, 'The angel Gabriel repeatedly informed me of the importance of the neighbor, so much so that I thought he would have him share in the inheritance.'"[8]

When the Christian mother of Al-Harith ibn Abi Rabi'a died, the Prophet 's companions participated in her funeral ceremony.[9]

Some prominent followers of the Prophet's companions used to give their *'Eid Al-Fitr* alms to Christian monks without any hesitation. Some of them, such as 'Ikrimah, Ibn Sirin, and Az-Zuhri even allowed the *zakah* to be given to Christians.

Ibn Abi Shiba reported on the authority of Jabir Ibn Zaid that he was once asked about the beneficiaries of *sadaqah* (alms). He said, "Give it to your Muslim brethren and non-Muslims."[10]

Qadi 'Ayad in his *Tartib Al-Madarik* said, Ad-Daraqutni related that Qadi

---

[6]Abu Yusuf, *Al-Kharaj*, p. 26. Also see my *Fiqh Az-Zakah*, Vol. II, pp. 705-706.
[7]Related by Imam Al-Bukhari in his *Sahih* and Yahya Ibn Adam in *Al-Kharaj*, p.44, and Al-Baihaqi in *As-Sunan*, Vol. IX, p. 206, "Bab Al-Wusat Bi Ahl Al-Kitab."
[8]Related by Imams Al-Bukhari, Muslim, Ahmad, Abu Dawud, and At-Tirmidhi.
[9]*Ibid.*,Chapter "Fiqh Az-Zakat."
[10]Ibn Hazm, *Al-Muhalla*, Vol. V, p. 117.

Isma'il ibn Ishaq[11] was once visited by Abdun ibn Sa'id, a Christian minister of the 'Abbasid *caliph* Al-Mu'tasim Billah. The *qadi* stood up and welcomed him warmly, an action not appreciated by his retinue. When the minister left, Qadi Isma'il said, 'I knew of your anger,' and then quoted the *Qur'an*:

> God forbids you not, with regard to those who fight you not for (your) faith, nor drive you out of your homes, from dealing kindly and justly. (Al-Mumtahana: 8)

This was the kind and just attitude ordained by Allah in the *Qur'an* . This tolerance is also evident in the attitudes of many *imams* and *fuqaha'* who defended non-Muslims and considered their honor and respect like those of Muslims. We have already mentioned the attitudes of Imam Al-Auza' and Imam Ibn Taimiyyah in this regard.

In this context, we shall quote the much respected theologian and scholar of jurisprudence, Shihab ad-Din al-Qarafi. His explanation of the righteousness with which Allah ordered the Muslims to conduct their affairs is as follows:

> This righteousness consists in being gentle with those who are weak among the non-Muslims: in helping their needy; in feeding their hungry; in clothing their destitute; in speaking to them with kindness and compassion rather than striking fear into them or humiliating them; in bearing with their harm, in exercising benevolence with courage, in showing no fear; in praying for guidance for them as well as for their prosperity. This attitude furthermore consists in seeking their welfare in all matters; in their religion and affairs of this world; in abstaining from slandering them should somebody attempt to harm them; in protecting their honor as well as all their rights and interests; in supporting them against aggressors; in ensuring the fulfillment of all their rights ...[12]

Ideological Basis of Muslim Tolerance

The tolerance evident in Muslims' relations with non-Muslims can be traced to certain truths which Islam inculcates into their minds and hearts. Among the most important of these are:

1) That every Muslim respects and believes in the dignity of mankind, regardless of religion, nationality, or color. Allah says :

"We have honored the sons of 'Adam." (Al-Isra': 70)

It is this divinely ordained honor which gives every human being the right of

---

[11] A Maliki intellectual, *qadi* of Bagadad, who died in 282 AH. For his brief account, see *Tartib Al-Madarik*, Vol. III, pp. 116-188, ed. Dar Al-Hayat, Beirut. Researched by Ahmad Bukair Mahmoud.
[12] *Al-Furuq*, Vol. III, p. 15.

respect and dignity. We have already cited practical examples in this regard, such as the *hadith* related by Imam Al-Bukhari on the authority of Jabir Ibn 'Abdullah that the Prophet stood up upon seeing a funeral procession. When he was told that the deceased was a Jew, he said, "Is it not a human soul?!"

In Islam, every soul has its dignity and its place. How gracious was the Prophet's attitude and what a beautiful lesson there was in his noble retort.

2) Muslims believe that differences of religion between people are a matter of divine decision. Allah says:

Let him who will, believe, and let him who will, reject (it). Al-Kahf: 29)

If your Lord had so willed, He could have made mankind one people, but they will not cease to dispute. (Hud: 118)

Muslims are convinced that Allah's will is beyond challenge. He wills only what is beneficial and just for mankind, whether they know it or not. Thus, a Muslim does not entertain thoughts of forcing others to embrace Islam, since Allah said to His Prophet:

If it had been your Lord's will, they would all have believed — all who are on earth! Will you then compel mankind against their will to believe?! (Yunus: 99)

3) It is not the duty of a Muslim to call the non-believers to account for their disbelief, nor to punish those who go astray for their errors. This world is not a place of judgment, for on the Last Day Allah will call them to account: on that day He will requite them. Allah says:

If they do wrangle with you, say: God knows best what you are doing. God will judge between you on the Day of Judgment concerning the matters in which you differ. (Al-Hajj: 68-69)

Allah addresses His Prophet concerning the *people of the book* in the following manner:

Now, then, for that (reason), call (them to faith), and stand steadfast as you are commanded, nor follow their vain desires, but say: 'I believe in the Book which God has sent down, and I am commanded to judge justly between you. God is our Lord and your Lord. For us (is the responsibility for) our deeds and for you for your deeds. There is no contention between us and you. God will bring us together. And to Him is (our) final goal. (Ash-Shur a: 15)

Through this belief, a Muslim gains peace of mind: there is no conflict within him between his belief and the disbelief of the infidel, nor between his duty to act with equity toward the non-believer and his own religious and doctrinal convictions.

4) A Muslim believes that Allah has ordained justice and the best of morals, even for polytheists. He hates opposition and cruelty, and punishes oppressors, even though the oppressor be a Muslim. Allah says:

"And let not the hatred of others for you make you swerve to wrong and depart from justice. Be just: that is next to piety." (Al-Ma'idah: 9)

The Prophet said, "The supplication of an oppressed person, even though he be a pagan, is heard directly, without any veil."[13]

---

[13]Related by Imam Ahmad in his *Musnad*.

IV / History As A Witness

History is witness to the fact that constitutions and laws are framed, enshrining the noblest ideals of mankind; but seldom do they go beyond their theoretical formulation.

Conscious of the fact that Islamic laws are divine in origin, Muslims accepted and applied them to an extent that has no parallel in the history of mankind. Their just treatment of other faiths is no secret. Concerning the Ummayad and 'Abassid periods, Will Durant says in his *The Story of Civilization:*

> To these *Dhimmi* — Christians, Zoroastrians, Sabaeans, Jews — the Umayyad caliphate offered a degree of toleration hardly equaled in contemporary Christian lands. They were allowed the free practice of their faiths, and the retention of their churches, on condition that they wear a distinctive honey-colored dress, and pay a poll tax of from one to four dinars ($4.75 to $19.00) per year according to their income. This tax fell only upon non-Moslems capable of military service; it was not levied upon monks, women, adolescents, slaves, the old, crippled, blind, or very poor. In return the *dhimmi* were excused (or excluded) from military service, were exempt from the two and a half per cent tax for community charity, and received the protection of the government. Their testimony was not admitted in Moslem courts, but they were allowed self-government under their own leaders, judges, and laws ...

> Christian heretics persecuted by the patriarchs of Constantinople, Jerusalem, Alexandria, or Antioch were now free and safe under a Moslem rule that found their disputes quite unintelligible. In the ninth century, the Moslem governor of Antioch appointed a special guard to keep Christian sects from massacring one another at church. Monasteries and nunneries flourished under the skeptical Umayyads; the Arabs admired the work of the monks in agriculture and reclamation, acclaimed the wines of monastic vintage, and enjoyed, in traveling, the shade and hospitality of Christian cloisters. For a time relations between the two religions were so genial that Christians wearing crosses on their breasts conversed in mosques with Moslem friends. The Mohammedan bureaucracy had hundreds of Christian employees; Christians rose so frequently to high office as to provoke Moslem

complaints. Sergius, father of St. John of Damascus, was chief finance minister to Abd-al-Malik, and John himself, last of the Greek Fathers of the Church, headed the council that governed Damascus. The Christians of the East in general regarded Islamic rule as a lesser evil than that of the Byzantine government and church.

Despite, or because of this policy of tolerance in early Islam, the new faith won over to itself in time most of the Christians, nearly all the Zoroastrians and pagans, and many of the Jews, of Asia, Egypt, and North Africa.[1]

As to the situation during the 'Abbasid period, the golden age for Islamic civilization, Kharbutali says:

In the 'Abbasid age several non-Muslim dignitaries had enormous reputations, one being Jarzia ibn Bakhtishu', the physician of the 'Abbasid *caliph* Abu Ja'far al-Mansur. The *caliph* was well satisfied with him and honored him generously. Then there was also Jibril Ibn Bakhtishu', the physician of the *caliph* Harun ar-Rashid, who said about Jibril: 'Anyone who wants to seek my help should contact Jibril, because I do whatever he asks of me and requests from me.' A physician's monthly salary was at that time 10,000 *dirhams*. Masaweih, one of Harun ar-Rashid's physicians, received 1,000 *dirhams* annually, and, at the end of every year, 20,000 more.[2]

Asserting the tolerance of Muslims, Tritton[3] says:

Muslim writers are generous in recognizing the merit of these men who did not follow their religion. Hunain, who lived in the time of Mamun, is called the leader of his day in medicine. Hibatullah b. Tilmidh was 'the Hippocrates of his age and the Galen of his day.' Ibn Khallikan wonders that a man of his intelligence did not accept Islam. His contemporary, Abul Barakat Hibatulla, the Jew, was called the 'solitare of the age.'

When Salamaweih was ill, Mu'tasim sent his son to visit him, and when he died had the funeral service celebrated in the palace, with candles and incense in his presence, after the manner of the Christians. The caliph also fasted for a day.

Yuhanna born Masaweih served the caliphs from Rashid to Mutawakkil,

---

[1]Durant, Will, *The Story of Civilization: The Age of Faith* (Vol. IV) (New York: Simon and Schuster: 1950), pp. 218-219.

[2]Kharbutali, Hasan Ali, *Islam and Ahl Adh-Dhimma*

[3]Tritton, Arthur Stanley, *The Caliphs and Their Non-Muslim Subjects* (London: Frank Cass & Co., Ltd.), pp. 159, 160, 163, 164.

and was always present at their meal times. He was enough of a favorite with Mutawakkil to be allowed to chaff him mildly. He could also make jokes at the expense of Islam, jokes recorded by Muslim writers. To a priest who suffered from indigestion, and had tried all the remedies the doctor could recommend, he said, 'Turn Muslim; this is good for the digestion.' When 'Isa (b. Ibrahim b. Nuh), the secretary of Al-Fath (born Al-Khakah) turned Muslim, Yuhanna came home from the palace to find some monks in his house, and said to them, 'Get out of my house, children of sin. Turn Muslim, for the Messiah has just turned Muslim.'

During the first and second centuries relations between the Arabs and their subjects in the sphere of letters and arts were very friendly, and even in later times much of the old friendliness endured. It has been pointed out elsewhere that the government employed non-Muslims as engineers and architects.

In addition, Tritton says that during the first and second centuries of the *hijrah*, the Arabs had good relations with their subjects in the Arts. These relations were founded upon kindness. The Islamic state employed engineers and various workers who were non-Muslims. Many non-Muslims pursued their studies under Muslim scholars and *fuqaha'*. For example, Huna in Ibn Ishaq studied under Khalil ibn Ahmad and Sibaweh, to the extent that his word became the definitive reference in Arabic.[4] Yahya ibn 'Adi ibn Humaid , a scholar of profound knowledge in logics, studied under Al-Farabi. Thabit ibn Qurra studied under 'Ali ibn al-Walid and Mu'tazilah. He was the best calligrapher and a man of letters. His books and compilations prove that he was a man of profound thoughts and deep knowledge; he soon embraced Islam.[5]

The historian Tritton regards Ibrahim ibn Hilal, who attained a very high rank in the Islamic state, as a good example of 'Abbasid tolerance toward non-Muslims. Ibrahim served the state in several high positions, and was highly praised by poets.'Izz ad-Dawlah Bakhtiyar ibn Mu'izz ad-Dawlah al-Buwaihi even recommended that he be given a ministerial portfolio, provided he embraced Islam. (He never did). His dealings with Muslims were highly ethical, as he was honest and virtuous in his religion. There was correspondence between him and As-Sahib Isma'il ibn 'Abbad and Ash-Sharif ar-Razi, although they followed different doctrines. Ibrahim, moreover, learned the *Qur'an* by heart.

Muslim writers evinced keen interest in religious sects and denominations.

---

[4]Al-Asfahani, *Kitab Al-Aghani*, Vol. VIII, p. 136, in footnote.
[5]Ibn Abi Usaibi'a, *Tabaqat Al-Atibba'*, Vol. I, p. 185.

Ibn Hazm al-Andalusi (456 AH/1064 AD) was well acquainted with the Gospels and with Christian theology. Ibn Khaldun was well-versed in the Gospels and was familiar with Christian organizations, some of which he discussed in his *Muqaddimah*. Al-Qalqashandi believed that a writer should know the non-Muslims' religious festivals and ceremonies. Al-Maqrizi has described in detail the festivals of the Jews and Christians, as well as their numerous sects and denominations. He also mentioned the names of the patriarchs of Alexandria. Al-Qazwini and Al-Mas'udi have enumerated the sects of non-Muslims as mentioned in Al-Mas'udi's *At-Tanbih Wa Al-Ishraf*.

Elaborating upon the tolerance of Muslim rulers, Tritton says that Muslim rulers frequently went beyond what was required of them in their relations with non-Muslims. To make his point, he cites the presence of many churches and other (non-Muslim) places of worship in purely Arab (Muslim) cities. Government departments always had Christian and Jewish officials who were sometimes given very sensitive and influential posts. Some non-Muslims thus acquired great wealth. In addition, Muslims were accustomed to participating in Christian festivals.

V / Misrepresenting Islam

We will now deal with some of the allegations made by certain orientalists against Islam on this subject.

The Problem of Jizyah

One of the problems raised by missionaries and orientalists is the imposition of the *jizyah* on all non-Muslims. This institution has been so misinterpreted and misexplained that even the non-Muslims feel that it is some kind of religious-based discrimination against them. This is not the case. All the *jizyah* amounts to is a financial obligation placed upon those who do not have to pay the *zakah*. As the ratio of these two taxes is the same, it is obvious that the *jizyah* is simply a technique used by Islamic governments to make sure that everyone pays his fair share. If the term "*jizyah*" is too offensive to non-Muslims, it can always be changed : 'Umar ibn al-Khattab levied the *jizyah* upon the Christians of the Bani Taghlib and called it *sadaqah* (alms) out of consideration for their feelings.[1]

The noted historian Sir Thomas W. Arnold in his *Call to Islam*, states:

> This tax was not imposed on the Christians, as some would have us think, as a penalty for their refusal to accept the Muslim faith, but was paid by them in common with the other *dhimmis* or non-Muslim subjects of the state whose religion precluded them from serving in the army, in return for the protection secured for them by the arms of the Musalmans. When the people of Hirah contributed the sum agreed upon, they expressly mentioned that they paid this *jizyah* on condition that 'the Muslims and their leader protect us from those who would oppress us, whether they be Muslims or others.'[2]

In his covenant with the people of certain cities near Al-Haira, Khalid ibn al-Walid recorded: "If we are able to protect you, we deserve the collection of *jizyah*; otherwise, we shall not offer you protection."[3]

The seriousness with which the Muslims took their covenants with the non-Muslims is well illustrated by the following incident. During the reign of the

---

[1]Al-Qaradawi, Yusuf, *Fiqh Az-Zakah*, Vol. I, pp. 98-104.
[2]Arnold, Sir Thomas W., *Call to Islam*, third ed., Nahda Library , pp. 79-81, Arabic translation by Dr. Hasan Nahrawi.
[3]*Ibid.*

second *caliph*, 'Umar ibn al-Khattab, the Roman emperor Heraclius raised a huge army to repel the Muslim forces. It was thus incumbent upon the Muslims to concentrate their efforts on the battle. When the commander of the Muslims, Abu 'Ubaidah, heard this news, he wrote to his officials in all occupied cities in Syria and ordered them to return the *jizyah* which had been levied in those cities. He also addressed the public saying, "We are returning your money because we know that the enemy has gathered troops. By the terms stipulated in the covenant, you have obliged us to protect you. However, since we are now unable to fulfill these conditions, we have returned to you what you paid to us. We shall abide by the terms agreed upon in the covenant, if Allah helps us to rout the enemy."[4] Thus, a huge amount was taken from the state treasury and returned to the Christians, making them very happy. They prayed for and blessed the Muslim commanders. They exclaimed, "May Allah help you to overcome your enemies and return you to us safely. If the enemy were in your place, they would never have returned anything to us, but rather they would have taken all our remaining property."[5]

The *jizyah* was also imposed on Muslim men who could afford to buy their way out of military service. If a Christian group elected to serve in the state's military forces, it was exempted from the *jizyah*. Historical examples of this abound: the Jarajima, a Christian tribe living near Antioch (now in Turkey), by undertaking to support the Muslims and to fight on the battle front, did not have to pay the *jizyah* and were entitled to a share of the captured booty.[6] When the Islamic conquests reached northern Persia in 22 A.H., a similar covenant was established with a tribe living on the boundaries of those territories. They were consequently exempted from *jizyah* in view of their military services.[7]

Other examples are to be found during the history of the Ottoman Empire: the Migaris, a group of Albanian Christians, were exempted from the *jizyah* for undertaking to watch and guard the mountain ranges of Cithaeron and Geraned (which stretch to the Gulf of Corinth). Christians who served as the vanguard of the Turkish army for road repairs, bridge construction and so on were exempted from the *kharaj*. As a reward, they were also provided with some lands, free of all taxes.[7] The Christians of Hydra were exempted when they agreed to supply a group of 250 strong men for the (Muslim) naval fleet.[9] The Armatolis, Christians from southern Romania, were also exempted from the tax,[9] for they constituted a vital element in the Turkish armed forces during the sixteenth and seventeenth centuries. The Mirdites, an Albanian Catholic clan who lived in the mountains of northern Scutari, were exempted on the condition that they would offer an armored battalion in wartime.[10] The jizyah was also not imposed on the Greek Christians who had supervised the building of

---

[4]At-Tabari, Vol. I, p. 2050.
[5]*Ibid.*
[6]Al-Baladhuri, p. 159.
[7]*Ibid.*.
[8]Marsigli, Vol. I, p. 86.
[9]Finlay, Vol VI, pp. 30-33.
[10]Lazar, p. 56.

viaducts[11], which carried water to Constantinople,[12]nor on those who guarded the ammunition in that city,[13] as just compensation for their services to the state. However, Egyptian Muslim peasants exempted from military service were still required to pay the *jizyah*.[14]

Branding the Necks of the Ahl Adh-Dhimma

Another of the so-called questionable practices was marking a non-Muslim's neck with a seal. The common misconceptions are as follows:
This branding was a common and permanent practice;
This practice was invented by the Muslims;
This practice was a way of humiliating and oppressing non-Muslims.

Historians such as Al-Ya'qubi, Tritton and others have refuted these assertions: "The necks of the non-Muslims were marked with a seal at the time of the collection of the *jizyah*. These seals were later broken."[15] (Al-Ya'qubi), "The Arabs should not in fact be considered responsible for this dubious practice, since they are no more than imitators of the Byzantines who indulged in it before them."[16] (Professor Tritton) and "The Muslims' policy of marking the necks of non-Muslims at the time they collected the *jizyah* , as applied by the Byzantines, does not portray oppression or humiliation, but was simply a means of knowing who had paid the *jizyah* and who had not. This was all the more practical since there was no system of printing at that time, which made it difficult to print out receipts for the payment of *jizyah*." (Dr. 'Ali Hasan al-Kharbutali).
This procedure is still followed during elections in certain African and Asian countries. The hand of the voter is stamped with an indelible seal which may not be removed for two days so that the voter is prevented from voting twice.

Fashions and Dresses of Dhimmis

Another problem is the specifying of certain garments to be worn by non-Muslims. Some orientalists say that 'Umar ibn al-Khattab formally forbade them to copy the Muslims in their dress, saddles, and shoes. It is further claimed that 'Umar stipulated that they had to stamp specific signs on their shoulders or in the middle of their bodies to distinguish themselves from Muslims. This practice has also been attributed to 'Umar ibn 'Abdul 'Aziz.
Certain orientalists have called 'Umar ibn al-khattab's actions on this issue

---

[11]De Lajanquiere, p. 14.
[12]These bridges were built on pillars, to bring drinking water to cities. This kind of bridge had been prevalent in the Roman Empire since the first century A.D.
[13]Thomas Smith, p. 324.
[14]Dorostamus, p. 326.
[15]Al-Ya'qubi, *Tarikh Al-Ya'qubi*, Vol. II, p. 130, quoted from *Islam and Ahl Adh-Dhimma*, p. 71.
[16]*The Caliphs and Their Non-Muslim Subjects*, p. 132.

into question. They have done so in spite of the fact that Muslim historians such as At-Tabari, Al-Baladhuri, Ibn al-Athir, Al-Ya'qubi and others make no explicit mention of these terms. How on earth did the translators extract this information from Arab texts which themselves do not contain it?

The preceding practice does not serve as a precedent, for it is no more than an order issued by the legal authority at that time regarding a specific matter for a particular society at a specific time. It need not be implemented if the common interest of the society changes.

This method of distinguishing between people according to their religion was necessary in those days, as there was no alternative method of distinguishing among them: there was no identity card which indicated the name, surname, religion, sex or denomination of an individual. It was thus the need to distinguish between people which made it necessary to issue such orders and decisions. The *fuqaha'* do not consider specific dress for non-Muslims to be a necessity, since other marks of identification are now possible.

Here we shall quote Kharbutali about the reasons behind a specific dress:[17]

> Even if we suppose, for instance, that such orders were issued by the two *caliphs* ('Umar ibn al-Khattab and 'Umar ibn 'Abdul 'Aziz), the practice is not offensive. It is a way to distinguish between the followers of different religions, especially in a period when there was no identity card to indicate the holder's nationality, religion, age, and other particulars. Special dress was thus the only means of indicating the religion of every person. The Muslim Arabs had their dress as did the Christians, Jews and Magians. If the orientalists consider this stipultion to be a manifestation of oppression, we would like to say to them that the so-called oppression in this form affected both Muslims and non-Muslims. If the *caliphs* had ordered Arabs and Muslims not to copy others, then it is logical to order non-Arabs and non-Muslims not to copy Arab Muslims.

Tritton has also discussed this practice. He is of the opinion [18] that the reason behind imposing specific dress was to make it easy to distinguish between Christians and Muslims. Abu Yusuf[19] and Ibn 'Abdul Hakam, both early writers whose books have come down to the present time, also believe this. We should observe that at the time of the Muslim conquest, there was no need for Muslims to compel Christians to wear a specific dress, because both parties had their own specific clothing. The need for these orders arose later when, as Islamic civilization continued to develop, the occupied nations began to imitate their conquerors' dress. Whatever the case may be, these edicts about the form and type of dress were infrequently implemented. Moreover, there is a difference between writing a law and implementing it. Most *caliphs* and Muslim rulers

---

[17]See *Islam and Ahl Adh-Dhimma*, p. 84-85.
[18]*The Caliphs and Their Non-Muslim Subjects*.
[19]*Islam and Ahl Adh-Dhimma*, pp 81-87.

pursued policies of tolerance, brotherhood, and equality. They did not stipulate the dress for non-Muslims, and no voices of complaint or protest were heard. These facts can be easily verified from reliable historical sources.

The Christian poet Al-Akhtal (d. 95 AH) used to enter 'Abdul Malik ibn Marwan's palace in a specific dress consisting of a robe with a silk amulet, a golden chain and cross around his neck, and a beard wet with wine.[20] The *caliph* always welcomed him warmly.

In the covenant signed in 98 AH with the Christians of Jarajima, who lived in the Syrian mountains, it was stipulated that they would wear Muslim dress.[21]

Abu Yusuf has described the non-Muslims dress as follows: "None of them *(dhimmis)* was allowed to imitate Muslims in dress, mount, or in general appearance." In this matter he relied on 'Umar ibn al-Khattab's dictum: "Their dress should be distinguished from that of the Muslims." Thus the practice is only a social means of distinguishing between people, just as today we observe that each profession in a society has its own specific dress.

Feelings of Animosity Against the Christians

The Muslim commitment to religious tolerance notwithstanding, the orientalists still point out some historical incidents which clearly show a deviation from the pattern. The truth is that such incidents, albeit isolated and clearly not the Islamic norm, did take place. What they fail to realize, however, is that any given incident occurs only as the result of certain previous actions of at least one party. In the following text we will discuss those factors which have been conveniently ignored by such critics.

Islamic tolerance provided non-Muslims with the opportunity to occupy the highest financial and administrative positions. In spite of this, non-Muslims treated them with contempt and arrogance. In this connection, Mitz states, "The movements opposing the Christians were directed against the domineering attitude of the non-Muslims toward Muslims."[22] Mitz also says, "Most of the turmoils that occurred between the Christians and Muslims in Egypt during earlier centuries were a direct result of the tyrannical behavior of the Coptic provincial governors."[23] Another reason for hatred was the tremendous amount of wealth in non-Muslim hands. This had a mainly negative impact on the Muslims, for they apparently felt that it had been accumulated by illegal and devious methods (most of this wealth was acquired by means of gifts and donations given to these people by the *caliphs* and provincial rulers). Thus, the feelings of anger arising from this situation were more akin to financial and class sentiments than to religious sentiments. This view is supported by Professor Arnold's example in his *Call to Islam*:

'Abdul Malik ibn Marwan selected a Christian named Athnas, from the

---

[20] *The Caliphs and Their Non-Muslim Subjects.*
[21] *Al-Kharaj*, p. 72.
[22] Al-Asfahani, *Al-Aghani*, Vol. V, p. 169. If it is true, it is more an illustration of the ruler's carelessness than of his tolerance.
[23] Al-Baladhuri, *Futuh Al-Buldan*, p. 161.

city of Arha, as a tutor for his brother, 'Abdul 'Aziz. Athnas accompanied his pupil to Egypt when the latter became a provincial ruler there. It seems that Athnas used his royal connections and amassed a great fortune. It is said that he owned four thousand slaves, many buildings, farms, and quantities of silver and gold (as abundant 'as though they were pebbles' according to Arnold). His sons used to take one *dinar* from every soldier's monthly salary. The Egyptian army was made up of as many as 30,000 men in those days, so it is possible to have an idea about the great deal of wealth that he collected during his twenty-one years in that country.[24]

He also states:

Christian physicians in particular often amassed huge fortunes. They earned a great reputation in the houses of high-ranking officials. Jibril, the Nesotrian Christian physician who was appointed by the *caliph* Harun ar-Rashid as his personal physician, had an annual income of around 800,000 *dirhams* from his own properties, in addition to his annual salary, estimated at 280,000 *dirhams*, for his services to the *caliph*. The second physician, also a Christian, had an annual salary estimated at 22,000 *dirhams*. The Christians had gathered huge quantities of wealth from their businesses in commerce and industry. In fact, this wealth exerted a powerful influence on the masses and caused some Muslims to oppress them or to exert religious pressures on them.[25]

Yet another reason for these incidents is the fact that some Christians openly expressed their pleasure at the Christian Romans' victory over the Muslim army. This attitude naturally led to an outbreak of public fury against them, as it would in any country.

It cannot be denied that there were some rulers who harshly oppressed the non-Muslims. However, such examples are rare. Moreover, this category of rulers often oppressed Muslims before oppressing Jews or Christians, since there were no formal limitations to their tyranny. Many unjust rulers behaved mildly with non-Muslims because of their covenant, while they oppressed their fellow Muslims. Shaikh Dardir, a Maliki scholar of Egypt and one of the most learned religious scholars at that time, relates that the rulers of his age showed respect for non-Muslims and gave them preference over Muslims. He said: "Would that Muslims were ten times less numerous than non-Muslims. Muslims were saying: 'It would be better if they (the rulers) laid the *jizyah* on us as they do on the Christians and Jews and let us be free as they let them be free.'"[26]

---

[24]*Islamic Civilization in the Fourth Century A.H.*, Vol. I, p. 106.
[25]*Ibid.*, p. 112.
[26]*Call to Islam*, pp. 81-82, 3rd ed.

Misunderstood References

Certain passages from the *Qur'an* and the *hadith* have been misinterpreted to lend support to various orientalists' claims that Islam is biased toward Jews, Christians, and other non-Muslims. Some of these passages are:

> Let not the believers take for friends or helpers unbelievers rather than believers; if any do that, in nothing will there be help from God, except by way of precaution, that you may guard yourselves from them. But God cautions you (to remember Him). (Al-'Imran: 28)

> O you who believe: Take not for friends unbelievers rather than believers: do you wish to offer God an open proof against yourselves? (An-Nisa': 144)

> To the hypocrites give the tidings that there is for them (but) a grievous penalty. Yea, to those who take for friends unbelievers rather than believers; is it honor they see among them? Nay, — All honor is with God. (An-Nisa': 138-139).

> O you who believe! Take not the Jews and the Christians for your friends and protectors. They are but friends and protectors to each other. He among you that turns to them (for friendship) is of them. Verily, God guides not a people unjust. Those in whose hearts is a disease — you see how eagerly they run about among them, saying: 'We do fear lest a change of fortune bring us disaster.' (Al-Ma'idah: 54-55)

> "O you who believe! Take not for protectors your fathers and your brothers if they love infidelity above Faith. If any of you do so, they do wrong." (At-Tawbah: 23)
> "You will not find any people who believe in God and the Last Day loving those who resist God and His Apostle, even though they were their fathers or their sons, or their brothers or their kindred." (Al-Mujadalah: 12)

> O you who believe! Take not my enemies and yours as friends (or protectors) — offering them (your) love, even though they have rejected the Truth that has come to you, and have (on the contrary) driven out the Prophet and yourselves (from your homes), (simply) because you believe in God your Lord! If you h ave come out to strive in My Way and to seek My Good Pleasure, (take them not as friends), holding secret converse of love (and friendship) with them, for I know full well all that you conceal and all that you reveal. And any of you that does this has strayed from the Straight Path. (Al-Mumtahanah: 1)

> God only forbids you with regard to those who fight you for (your)

Faith, and drive you out of your homes and support (others) in driving
you out from turning to them (for friendship and protection). It is such
as to turn to them (in these circumstances) that do wrong. (Al-Mum-
tahana: 9)

Some people have seen in these and similar verses a call to dissension and
harshness, as well as an encouragement to sever relations and to kindle hatred
and contempt toward non-Muslims, even though some of these non-Muslims
may be sincere supporters of the Muslims. The fact remains, however, that
whoever critically studies the said verses along with the period, reasons, and
context of their revelation would easily discover the following facts: 1) The said
behavior,that is, "not to take opponents as friends," refers specifically to non-
Muslim religious groups who actively work against Islam and Muslims, and not
to those who live in peace with their Muslim neighbors and colleagues. It is
considered essential for Muslims that their devotion and amity should be exclusively within the Muslim *ummah,* and not toward those who would harm them.
There exists no religious or any other system which approves of any of its active
members forsaking his own group in favor of another, or best owing his affection
upon another group; 2) The amity which is prohibited is not the relationship of
cordiality, but rather the amity shown to those who harm Muslims and oppose
Allah and His Messenger. The "resistance" which is spoken of here not only
implies their nonbelief in Allah, but also their active opposition to the call and
spread of Islam, as well as their seeking harm to the believers. The reason for
the forbidding of friendships with polytheists was twofold: These people denied
Islam, and they unjustly expelled the Prophet and the Muslims from their homes.
Allah says:

God does not forbid you with regard to those who do not fight you for
(your) faith nor drive you out of your homes, from dealing kindly and
justly with them, for God loves those who are just. (Al-Mumtahanah: 8)

It is obvious that the *Qur'an* divides non-Muslims into two groups: those who
maintained peaceful relations with the Muslims, neither opposing nor expelling
them from their homes, and those who treated Muslims with aggression and
enmity, drove them from their homes, and helped their enemies to humiliate
them. This latter group, with whom the Muslims are not allowed to make friends,
includes the Makkan polytheists who severely tortured Muslims. Even a superficial reading of this verse shows that the former is not to be shunned; 3) Islam
allows Muslims to marry the women of the *people of the book.* Married life
should be peaceful, affectionate, and understanding:

"And among His Signs is this, that He created for you mates from
among yourselves, that you may dwell in tranquility with them, and He
has put love and mercy between your (hearts). (Ar-Rum: 21)

This proves that friendship between Muslims and non-Muslims is allowed.

How can one not be amiable with one's wife who is from the *people of the book*? How can a son not be amiable with his grandfather and grandmother, uncle and aunt, when his mother is a non-Muslim?; 4) The irrefutable fact is that Islam asserts religious ties above all other ties, whether of blood, territory, race, or any other category. So, a Muslim is the brother of another Muslim and together they all constitute one *ummah*. Every one of them has the same rights and responsibilities. They are all a unified body against others. A Muslim is closer to his Muslim fellows than to any non-believer, even though the latter may be his father, son, or brother. This attitude is not found only in Islam, but is a natural part of every religion and creed. Anyone who has studied the Gospels would find the confirmation of this statement in more than one situation.

[27] *Ibid.*, pp. 82-83.
[28] Ad-Dardir, *Ash-Sharh As-Saghir*, Vol. I, p. 269.

VI / A Comparative Study

Doubtless, Islamic tolerance is superior to that of other faiths. Nevertheless, if any evidence is called for, then one should make a comparative study of religions and see for himself the fate of those who refused to go along with the views of the majority. They should also look into the aftermath of the Muslim conquest of Andalusia and then compare that record with the Spanish Christians who reconquered it.

As a further proof of Islamic tolerance, they should study the lives of Muslim minorities under Christian, Hindu, or Communist rule, especially in an age which prides itself on upholding human rights. They should observe, for instance, the conditions of Muslims in Ethiopia — how they face oppression and violation of their human rights, even though they are the religious majority in several provinces.[1] They should examine the plight of the Muslims in the Soviet Union,[2] Yugoslavia, China, and other Marxist and socialist countries. Muslims in some of the Soviet republics, as well as in some Yugoslavian provinces, are in majority; yet, they are not allowed to observe the five daily prayers, nor the great majority of them is allowed to make the pilgrimage to the Sacred House of Allah in Makkah. They are neither allowed to study Islamic jurisprudence nor to seek the implementation of the *shari'ah* in the affairs of their community. Also prohibited is the construction of mosques and the creation of Islamic institutes to provide their communities with trained *imams*, teachers and *khutaba'* (those who deliver the Friday sermons) to meet their spiritual needs.

One would be incapable of appreciating Islam's contribution to humanity in the areas of ideological and religious tolerance unless he were to study those proposals advanced by modern secular creeds or ideologies in this domain.

Oppression, harshness, torture, murder, slaughter, collective annihilation, and constant terrorism do not allow tolerance to survive for any length of time. These actions are neither rare nor the result of special circumstances requiring special measures. Ruthless oppression of opponents is based on a certain theoretical philosophy which justifies violence as one of the necessities of any

---

[1] See *The Tragedy of Injured Islam in Ethiopia* and the report of two Azhari students from Ethiopia about the Muslims' conditions in that country, which was published by Shaikh Muhammad Al-Ghazali in his book *The Struggle of Religion*, under the title *Wolves of Ethiopia Tear Islam*. See also *Eriteria and Ethiopia* from the series of Mahmoud Shakir (published by Al-Aqsa Library, Amman, Jordan).

[2] See the chapter "Status Quo of Muslims in theU.S.S.R." from the book *Islam in the Face of the Red March* by Shaikh Muhammad Al-Ghazali.

revolution.[3] They further believe that such violence is the characteristic of every historical and contemporary religious or non-religious call. They think that violence should always be rigorously imposed so that it helps in behavior modification of the masses.

An observer of modern secular ideology says:

> Violence is usually exercised individually before taking charge of a government. Its purpose, as described by anarchists, especially the Russian anarchists, is to intimidate and disunite governmental authorities through fear,and to pave the way for the next step, that is, to seize power. But, after seizing power,this violence turns into a public violence aimed at establishing power instead of dismantling it. So, while individual violence is directed toward individuals in significant positions, this new revolutionary public violence is turned upon the people as a whole, or toward a specific group.This latter form of violence does not simply seek to intimidate its victims, but seeks their annihilation so that the society may be in harmony with the new ideology."[4]

The Communists in Russia unleashed inconceivable terror after the success of their revolution. The situation was so grave that even some of Lenin's assistants complained about the bloodshed caused by the civil war. When they asked Lenin about these human victims, he replied plainly: "It would not have mattered if even three-fourths of the human race had perished. Our only concern is that the surviving quarter becomes Communists."[5] The horrible massacres, bloodshed, and incessant purges under Stalin received a tremendous amount of media coverage during Khrushchev's reign. Such events are so well known that we feel no need to discuss them any further.[6]

The important fact is that the advocates of revolutionary violence justify their use of violence and harshness toward their opponents by falling back upon the history of religions which is itself replete with examples of oppression and the

---

[3]The philosophy of Communist revolutionaries and other similar views are based on the theory that violence is essential for revolutionary culture and the protection of the revolutionary dynamic and its purity. This so-called dynamic movement depends on violence to awaken the people from their sleep, constantly agitating them in order to keep them always on the move, and continually stirring their inner revolutionary consciousness. This violence seeks to ingrain the revolution in the consciousness of the people so that it is never forgotten. In other words, it is a means of preventing people from regarding the revolution as a tradition without consciousness, which would of course mean the end of the revolution! See Al-Bittar, Nadim,*Revolutionary Ideology*, chapter "Revolutionary Violence," p. 701.

[4]Al-Bittar, Nadim, *Revolutionary Ideology*, published by the Al-Ahlia Foundation for Printing and Distribution, Beirut, pp. 706-707.

[5]*Ibid.*, p. 688.

[6]See the speech of Khrushchev during the 20th Conference of the Communist Party. Translated by Mahir Nasim with a preface by Professor Abbas Al-'Aqqad. Printed by the Anglo-Egyptian Library, Ar-Risala Press.

annihilation of those who dared to disagree. These modern revolutionaries cite the history of Christianity during its early years and the Middle Ages and claim that the Nazis and Communists learned organized violence from Jesuit-headed Christian schools and the Inquisition. Christianity calls for love and peace, but when it was the dominant power, in the form of a state entity, it subjected those who believed differently to severe torture and mistreatment.

In his *Islam and Christianity*, Sheikh Muhammad 'Abduh states:

> The Spanish Church became extremely concerned by the spread of Ibn Rushd's philosophy, especially among the Jews.
> Both Jews and Muslims were subjected to torture to forsake their faiths. First Jews were given baptism. Those who refused were forced to sell their properties and leave Spain, provided they did not carry on their person precious metals such as gold and silver. Perhaps many died on their way out of Spain.
> In 1052 A.D., the Church ordered the expulsion of Muslims (the so-called enemies of God) from Ishbilia and the surrounding area, because they too refused baptism. They were directed not to take a route which led to Islamic countries. Anyone caught opposing these orders was killed.[7]

This oppression was not only directed toward atheists and members of different faiths, but also toward those Christians who had opinions or doctrines contrary to the beliefs of the rulers or the Church. Those who have studied Christian history are aware of how the Egyptian intellectual Arius and his followers were dealt with by the famous Council of Nicea in 325 A.D. for rejecting the divinity of Jesus. This Council, after expelling all opposition members, decided to condemn Arius, and to ban and burn his writings. Those who supported him were fired from their positions, sent into exile, and subject to execution if they retained any of Arius' writings or continued to support his ideology. Because of such oppression, the Unitarians totally disappeared from Christian societies; nothing remained of their beliefs or claims.[8]

Some writers have explained:

> The theological differences among Christians regarding certain utterances of the New Testament (*Injil*) led to fatal conflicts such as: whether the emanation of the Holy Spirit was from the Father and the Son or from the Son only; whether or not bread and wine represented the body and blood of Jesus; whether Jesus possessed two natures (human and divine) or not, and so on. It is clear that these principles were all disputable matters. The Unitarians challenged their fellow Christians on such issues and suffered great tortures.

---

[7] *Islam and Christianity with Science and Civilization*, pp. 36-37, 8th ed.
[8] *Revolutionary Ideology*, p. 714.

When the Protestant school appeared in Europe under the leadership of Luther and others, the Catholic Church opposed it with everything at their disposal. This history of oppression with all of its horrifying massacre is well known. The most famous incident of this conflict is the Paris Massacre of August 24, 1572. The Catholics, having invited the Protestants to Paris for a mutual airing of their differences and possible compromises, fell upon their guests and murdered them while they were sleeping. When the sun rose the following day, Protestant blood was flowing in the streets of Paris. The Catholic Pope, kings and high ranking officials warmly praised King Charles IX for this deed. But it is also surprising that when the Protestants gained power, they requited the Catholics with an eye for an eye, showing no less brutality than the Catholics had.[9]

Luther said to his followers: "You should kill, strangle, slaughter and do whatever you can to those revolutionary peasants."[10] It is hardly surprising that Europe's religious wars were so atrocious. Fiark says that in Germany the religiously-oriented Thirty Years War (fought between 1618-1648) destroyed most of the German people through death and hunger; they tore down or burned many cities to ashes.

The Crusades were so horrible that the revolutionary experiments of the twentieth century (such as those of the Nazis and the Communists) can in no way compete with the inter-Christian massacres of the past. It is noteworthy that some of them ploughed their lands using their victims' remains as fertilizer.

Feedham says:

> The history of these raids and wars abounds with horrible deeds. Since the 'virtuous' theologians were always ready to add fuel to the fire, they goaded soldiers to commit atrocities when they felt any weakness or confusion. Though the soldiers took rigorous measures, they were sometimes gentle and merciful, whereas the theologians considered moderation and mercy with those people to be a sort of treachery.[11]

A perceptive observer of medieval Christianity says:

> The main purpose of Christianity, like every revolutionary ideology, was to create a Christian world, exclusively populated by Christian believers. Being of the Christian faith was an essential condition for an individual to become a member of society in the Middle Ages; it was also a necessity to be able to possess that nationality. Thus the Jews, pagans, and Muslims were socially ostracized, and their rights were totally denied.

---

[9]See *Christianity*, by Dr. Ahmad Shalab, pp. 51-52.
[10]*Revolutionary Ideology*, p. 710.
[11]*Ibid.*, p. 716.

In its early stages Christianity resorted to all methods of coercion to spread itself, (such as acceptance of baptism or death). It later resorted to missionary work in order to realize its objects.

The Crusades are a living example of Christianity's spread. In the period between the eleventh and fourteenth centuries they showed no reticence in attempting to achieve their goal of turning the entire world into a Christian world by annihilating non-Christian nations. This aim appeared in the *Song of Roland*, a medieval epic poem which expresses the essence of the First Crusade. It is clear from this epic that the pagans were being coerced to accept baptism, and that those who did not were either hanged, crucified, or beheaded.

These Crusades were not aimed at the Muslims alone, but also at those who wanted to abandon or change the Church in Europe. The Church, in the twelfth and thirteenth centuries AD, directed its campaigns against the Catharis, the Waldenses, and the Albigenses in an attempt to annihilate them. This is precisely what the Church achieved. Through arson and murder it massacred multitudes of men, women, and children.

Lee, in his classic study of the Inquisition's Courts, says:

All courts and judges were required to solemnly swear, on pain of losing their positions, to eradicate those whom the Church considered renegades. If any governor, ordered by the Church to purge his land of renegades, neglected to fulfill the prescribed task for one year, his land was given to anyone who undertook to annihilate them. These courts instituted a special "decree of faith" whereby renegades were persecuted and people declared subservient to the courts. People were asked to spy on each other and inform the establishment of the activities of any renegade or pagan.[12]

"The Inquisition Courts," Sheikh Muhammad 'Abduh says, were so extreme that it became impossible for a Christian to die a natural death in his own bed," and that "Since their inception in 1481 AD until 1808 AD, the Inquisition Courts executed 340,000 people, 200,000 of whom were burned alive."[13]
This attitude was not a new thing in Christianity. In its earliest years Christianity propagated itself largely through coercion or threat of capital punishment. Brifault mentions that historians estimate the number of people killed by Christianity during its propagation throughout Europe to be between seven and fifteen million.[14] The persecutors believed that they were exercising a divine obligation

---

[12] *Revolutionary Ideology*, pp. 586-588.
[13] *Ibid.*, p. 715.
[14] *Islam and Christianity with Science and Civilization.*

and pleasing God by torturing His enemies with certain forms of punishment which awaited them on the Day of Final Judgment. Queen Mary, one of the Catholic rulers of England during the sixteenth century AD, expressed this very belief by declaring: "Since the souls of unbelievers will burn in Hell forever, there is nothing more legal than to imitate and pursue divine retribution — that is to burn them on earth."[15]

Writing on this topic, Bori states:

> ... the Church introduced a principle into common European laws by which the king or the prince could exercise his authority on one basis: annihilation of any party which opposes the Church. Thus, if anybody opposed the Church by even hesitating to obey its orders, the Church transferred his land and possessions to any person whom it deemed fit. This was done as a measure of coercion.

He states in another place:

> The Roman oppression of Christians stems from Christian fanaticism and its contradiction of all religions, as well as from its enmity toward all forms of faith, and its belief that its success and victory would mean the eradication of all other ideologies.

It is this very phenomenon which made William Jayis state that the world did not know religious oppression on a wide scale before the appearance of the monotheistic religions. Christianity was the first religion in the world characterized by fanaticism. It did not hesitate to fight against schismatic movements to their total destruction. The desire then grew quite naturally in the persecuted. Thus forced by persecution, the dissidents sought alliance against the Church and hurt it when possible. Christianity, represented by its Church, would stake its claim against atheists outside the country on one hand and against renegades inside the country on the other. It organized the Crusades against the former and established Inquisition Courts for the latter. Burning at the stake was the punishment for all schismatic groups. A person who repented and confessed his mistake, begging for pardon, was sentenced to life imprisonment. All of the renegade's properties and belongings, along with those of his offspring, were confiscated until the following generation. They were not authorized to hold any position unless they denounced their fathers or other renegades. The same punishment was inflicted upon those who supported the renegades in any form. Even the deceased were not left untouched, for the Inquisition's officials ordered the exhumation and cremation of the bodies of those whom they suspected to be apostates. Encouragement to spy upon and to denounce others were brought to a point of fanaticism, unparalleled in the history of modern revolutionary movements.

---

[15]*Revolutionary Ideology*, p. 714.

Conclusion

This study, we hope, makes it clear that Islamic tolerance toward non-Muslims is an established fact, supported by the reigns of Prophet Muhammad's first four successors (known in history as the "Four Rightly-Guided Caliphs," — *al-khulafa' ar-rashidun*) and their successors: the 'Umayyad and 'Abbasid as well as the Ottoman, Mameluke, and other dynasties in many Islamic countries. This tolerance is still evident today in the Islamic world where churches are built side by side with mosques and where Muslims can hear the call of the *muezzin* as well as the peal of church bells. It is also evident that non-Muslim minorities live peacefully in Islamic societies without any infringement on their religious rights, while Muslim minorities and sometimes Muslim majorities ruled by non-Muslim governments in several Asian, African, and European countries are oppressed. They are not allowed to live according to their faith. On the contrary, Islam even prohibits the punishment of non-Muslims (who are under Muslim protection) for the crimes of their brethren in other countries, since they clearly have no complicity in their co-religionists' crimes. Allah says:

"Every soul draws the recompense of its acts on none but itself. No bearer of burdens can bear the burden of another." (Al-An'am: 164)

The fact is that Islam has a definite and unambiguous attitude toward non-Muslims.

We are nevertheless very much surprised to find western wiiters who try to distort Islam's image by falsifying actual history and then unjustly accusing Islam and Muslims of prejudice and fanaticism against the non-Muslim citizenry. Even UNESCO, supposedly an international and non-aligned organization partly supported by the generous contributions of Muslim countries, has published a book on the history of mankind which describes Islam and its history from the same unfair perspective: they accuse Islam of things it is innocent of. There are also some individuals who abuse and exploit the concept of tolerance so as to undermine Islam and promote chauvinism, nationalism, and other similar notions.

Muslims call for tolerance because Islam says so. This does not mean that Muslims should renounce Islam to please others. We do not compel others to leave their faith, so why should they compel us to leave ours?

It is not tolerance to force Muslims to abandon Allah's *shari'ah* for the sake of non-Muslim minorities whose feelings should supposedly be spared at all costs.

We do not understand why a Christian or a Jew should be so offended by the amputation of a thief's hand, or the flogging of slanderers, adulterers, and drunkards, or by any other punitive measures of the *shari'ah*, be he Muslim or non-Muslim. A Muslim adheres to these orders because for him it is an act of worship — a means of becoming closer to Allah. A non-Muslim, however, takes them to be no more than criminal laws adopted by the majority, thereby failing to understand their divine nature.

There cannot be any tolerance when relations between Muslims and Christians, for example, are established on the basis of hypocrisy, thereby giving precedence to relations of nationalism or chauvinism over those of faith. This is done in spite of the fact that such an idea contradicts both the letter and spirit of Islam and Christianity.

Tolerance must be realized according to both religious teachings, for instance, by implementing good mutual relations, the furtherance of common interests, and justice for all.

The rhetoric of the secular nationalists — "Religion is for God, and the land is for all" — is meaningless. This should be changed into "Religion is for Allah, and the land is for Allah," or "Religion is for all, and the land is for all," or "Religion is for all, and the land is for Allah."

Better, if expressions that neither enhance understanding, nor solve any problems are discarded. Moreover, they do not even provide the basis for any dialogue.

At the same time tolerance does not lie in ignoring fundamental differences between faiths to the extent of making the Oneness of God synonymous with the Trinity. Such an attitude enhances misunderstanding and leads to further fragmentation. Each religion has its own peculiarities, right or wrong.

True cooperation and harmony between faiths does not need superficial courtesies. "It is Allah who speaks the truth and guides us to the right path."

BIBLIOGRAPHY

'Abdul Karim Zaidan, *Ahkam Adh-Dhimmiyyin Wa Al-Musta'minin Fi Dar Al-Islam*.
'Abdul Malik ibn Sa'id, *Al-Laith*.
'Abdul Qadir 'Awdah, *Islamic Criminal Legislation*.
'Abdur Razaq, *Al-Musannaf*.
Abu 'Ubaid al-Qasim ibn Salam, *Al-Amwal*.
Abu Yusuf, *Al-Kharaj*.
Abul A'la al-Maududi, *Rights of Dhimmis in the Islamic State*.
Adam Mitz, *The Islamic Civilization in the Fourth Century A.H.* (translation by Muhammad 'Abdul Hadi Abn Rida).
Ad-Dardir, *Ash-Sharh As-Saghir*.
Ahmad ibn al-Hanbal, *Matalib ula An-Nuha*.
Ahmad Shalab, *Christianity*.
Al-Asfahani, *Kitab Al-Afghani*.
Al-Baladhuri, *Futh Al-Buldan*.
'Ali Hasan al-Kharbotaly, *Islam and Dhimmis*.
Al-Jasas, *Ahkam Al-Qur'an*.
Al-Kasani, *Al-Bada'i*.
Al-Ya'qubi, *Tarikh Al-Ya'qubi*.
Arthur Stanley Tritton, *The Caliph and Their Non-Muslim Subjects*.
As-Sarakhsi, *As-Siyar Al-Kabir*.
As-Suyuti, *Husn Al-Muhadara*.
At-Tabarani, *Al-Awsat*.
Baihaqi, *As-Sunan Al-Kubra*.
Gustave Lebon, *Arab Civilization* (translated by 'Adil Za'aytar).
Ibn al-Athir, *Faid Al-Qadir*.
Ibn 'Abidin, *Hashiyya Ibn 'Abidin*.
Ibn 'Abidin, *Ad-Durr Al-Mukhtar*.
Ibn Abi Usaibi'a, *Tabaqat Al-Atibba'*.
Ibn Abi Zaid, Ibn Naji and Zaruqi, *Risala and the Two Commentaries Upon It*.
Ibn 'Asakir, *History of Damascus*.
Ibn Hazm, *Al-Muhalla*.
Ibn Kathir, *Tafsir Ibn Kathir*.
Ibn Qayyim, *Za d Al-Ma'ad*.
Ibn Qudamah, *Al-Mughni*.
Ibn Sa'd, *Tarikh At-Tabari*.
Imam Al-Qarafi al-Malaki, *Al-Furuq*.
Imam Al-Hakim, *Al-Muntaqa*.
Nadim al-Bittar, *Revolutionary Ideology*.
Shaukani, *Nail Al-Awtar*.

Sheikh Muhammad 'Abduh, *Islam and Christianity With Science and Civilization*.
Sir Thomas Arnold, *Call To Islam* (translated by Dr. Hasan Nahrawi).
Yusuf al-Qaradawi, *Fiqh Az-Zakat*.
Will Durant, *The Story of Civilization: The Age of Faith* (Volume IV), Simon and Schuster, New York, N.Y.

INDEX

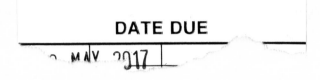